Legends
of the Crane

"This book—with retrospects from many of
the people who experience these birds every
year—captures the timeless legend of the crane.
The writers and artists are secure in knowing
that this legend will endure."

Pete Letheby, *The Grand Island Independent*

by
Pamela J. Jensen

Sandstones Press

Legends of the Crane
By Pamela J. Jensen
Copyright © 2000 by Pamela J. Jensen
All rights reserved
First edition 2000

LIBRARY OF CONGRESS CATALOG CARD NUMBER
99-97207
Jensen, Pamela J.
Legends of the Crane – 1st ed.
ISBN 0-9676879-0-X

Printed in Hong Kong by Colorcraft Ltd.
Cover design by Cambridge Writing & Editing
Book design by Cambridge Writing & Editing
Cover artwork, original oil painting by Doug Miller

To obtain limited, signed, and numbered prints of this cover artwork, contact Doug Miller, PO Box 1277, Ephrata, WA 98823

Dedication

Dedicated to my family,
Harry and Jewel Jensen and Lydia Camp,
and to the Nebraska migrating Sandhill Cranes.

There is a time for everything, and a season for every activity
under heaven.
—Ecclesiastics 3:1 NIV

Contents

Part Three

Part Four

Part Five

Part Six

List of Illustrations

Preface

CRANES HAVE BEEN on Earth for longer than almost any other living creature. Fossil records of cranes date back millions of years. No wonder they have been featured in so many stories and legends from around the world. A sad fact is that, in days of old, cranes were far more numerous than they are now and were familiar to many more people. As their natural habitats of swamps and marshlands are drained or otherwise destroyed, they have retreated to remote regions to nest and breed in the spring, and to special refuges where abundant food is provided in the winter. However, cranes are widespread globally, existing on five of the seven continents. Only Antarctica and South America do not have crane populations.

Biologically, cranes are considered to be large wading birds of the family *Gruidae*, having a long neck, long legs, and a long bill. Herons are similar to cranes, but they are classified as the major category or the major species of the family of wading birds *Ardeidae*. Egrets fall under the heron family. Storks are large wading birds of the family *Ciconiidae*. In spite of their differing families, all of these birds have not only developed common physical characteristics, but as wading birds, they have also evolved similar adaptations to living in the wetlands. Because of the similarities between their species, this book will include numerous short stories, poems, and artwork about all of them.

CRANES HAVE BEEN WIDELY depicted in both Chinese and Japanese art and literature as symbols of good fortune, happy marriage (the birds choose a single mate for life), longevity (a crane can live as many as eighty years in captivity), and immortality. Representations of cranes are popular in wedding ceremonies.

Reflecting the quality of nobility and superiority attributed to cranes, a crane motif was embroidered on the robes of first grade officials in Imperial China. Cranes were one of the emblems attached to the literary scholar in traditional Chinese thought, their graceful movements and dignified bearing appealing to the Chinese sense of propriety.

"Crane age" is a metaphor for a person of advanced years. Cranes are associated with and sometimes called the *hsien-jen*, the Immortals. Since cranes fly for long distances and at great heights,

it is said that the Immortals use the crane as their favorite mount. Many a holy recluse is said to have disappeared from human sight, riding on a crane. In a related vein, one Chinese custom is to place the figure of a crane with spread wings on a coffin (again, in association with the Immortals).

ALTHOUGH THE CRANE in its wild state is very wary of humans, there are many stories of cranes in captivity that become inseparable companions of men, and of cranes in the wild that show human understanding. Japan has many legends about cranes that were wounded or trapped but were finally saved by kindly peasants.

In Japan, one of the most popular ways of using the crane to represent happiness and peace is the art of folding paper into a bird, animal, or other form. This art is called origami, and nearly two hundred years ago, a book called *Sembazuru Orikata* (*Folding a Thousand Cranes*) was written about origami. Ever since, Japanese children have strung up chains of a thousand paper cranes they have folded to make their wishes come true, and their handiwork has taken on a religious significance. For example, thousands and thousands of paper cranes have been strung up as a prayer of peace and the outlawing of nuclear weapons.

ON THE OTHER SIDE of the ocean, the crane has played an important part in the cultural religious life of many Native American tribes from earliest times. Cranes frequently appear in tribal art—from ancient paintings on stone to modern craftwork using crane motifs. Clan totems can be a representation of birds, animals, fish, or reptiles, and the crane is prominent among the bird totems adopted. Other favored choices include the eagle, the gull, the goose, and the hawk. For members of the Crane Clan, the crane itself and crane feathers used in some festive or religious ceremonies have particular significance. The names Crane Island, Crane Creek, Crane Lake, and Crane Valley occurred in widespread parts of Canada and United States, showing that in the past these birds were familiar visitor—even in places where they are rarely seen today.

CRANES ARE AMONG THE finest dancers of the bird world. Males and females bow and leap when courting, but whole flocks of cranes have been observed dancing rhythmically, apparently for the sheer joy of the movement. Human dances based on the expressive movements of cranes are found in Japan, Africa, and even Australia. The Chinese lute, a seven-stringed musical instrument over two thousand years old, is still played. Cranes are mentioned in connection with the playing of this instrument, because both present graceful movements and dignified behavior. It is said that lutes are used to make cranes dance, and in order to play the lute properly, one should first dress correctly—either in a gown of crane feathers or a ceremonial robe.

SOME OF THE OLDEST stories and poems in human culture come from China and Japan where the crane is held in special veneration. In these fables, stories, and poems, cranes are clever, resourceful, and affectionate, but it is their proud grace and beauty that make them so beloved. As you read the following stories and poems, you may notice that some of them do no more than mention cranes, herons, egrets, or storks. Go beyond the mere mention. Go deeper. Read, feel, and experience the descriptions of rivers, islands, hills, sandbars, and sky—their habitat. (Part of the experience of reading *Legends of the Crane* will include the challenge of reading old English verbiage as it was originally translated—and spelled.)

FINALLY, (it cannot be said often enough) to have had such a wonderful caliber of talent involved in the compilation of this book has been a great honor! You know who you are...

Pamela J. Jensen
January 2000

Part One

The Sandhill Cranes

THE CRANES ARE FLYING THROUGH THE AIR
In just precise formation
Reminding man that they're a part
Of God's immense creation

Their spirits never knew a cage
Or what it's like to cater
To forces other than that given
By the divine Creator

Soaring high gracefully in flight
Seemingly effortless they journey on
Seeking refuge for the night
Their destination they have flown

Their music with earth's symphony harmonize
With blowing winds and shifting sand
While migration instructs they realize
It's all a mystery to mere man

They cover the fields of valleys and ranches
To glean the grain they find by chances
Remnants of harvest left last fall
Of barley, wheat, oats and all

So very scarce the whooping crane
Endangered species so they claim
The white among the gray is plain
Experts working frantically to reclaim

Interesting to watch their courting gyrations
Hopping, jumping and flopping of wings
Nature's wonders need no explanation
We take for granted these natural things

In the spring, time here is short at best
As food supply is soon depleted
We celebrate their presence with fest
Next fall their visit is repeated

They return then in the fall
The coffers full and running over
It's most certain they have a ball
Sure they're basking in the clover

When airborne they form a V
The navigator his flock he leads
That of its self is great to see
He knows that he has met their needs

In their own time farther south they go
Soaring high in the Azure sky
To warmer sights as well they know
Until next spring we say goodbye.

—Georgia McGuire

From *Ch'ang-ku*

MOSS-COINS, STREWN, THICKLY CUSHION ROCKS,
Full leaves bunch in heavy clusters.
Smooth and white lie water-rinsed sands,
Where the horse stands, hooves print dark signs.
As evening comes, bright scales grow playful here,
A thin crane stands alone, immobile in the dusk.

—Li Ho
from *Sunflower Splendor,*
Three Thousand Years of Chinese Poetry

Ch'ang-ku is the township in which Li Ho's family home was
located, about 50 miles southwest of Lo-yang.

The Gifts of the Cranes

THERE IS A WONDERFUL old tradition in some parts of Scan-
dinavia in which the children hang their stockings outside
their houses during those days in early spring when the European
cranes first return from their wintering areas in France and Spain.
Sometimes the children may place an ear of corn or some other
gift to pass on to the cranes, whose welcome voices and overhead
flocks are the surest sign of spring and renewed hope for the future after enduring a long, unbearably dark, and frigid Scandina-
vian winter. In return, the birds may leave a gift of their own for
the children before they pass still farther northward to their remote sub-arctic breeding grounds. It's a tradition I would love to
see started in North America, perhaps as a substitute for what I
regard as the rather silly Easter bunny-Easter egg tradition. As an
ornithologist I have a good deal of trouble thinking that even
children can believe that rabbits might actually produce and deliver dyed bird eggs or their candy versions. Yet I think it was no
less a personage than the White Queen who admitted that she
liked to think of at least six impossible things before breakfast,

and so egg-bearing rabbits are perhaps better than everyday television in enriching the distinctive baby voices to remain in touch with imaginary lives of children.

Speaking of unbelievable things, it is unbelievable that so many Nebraskans have yet to make what is for me an annual religious pilgrimage to the Platte Valley each spring, to revel in the sounds and sights of uncountable cranes and geese, and to know that the promise of another Nebraska spring has been fulfilled by their simple presence. The splendor of several thousand cranes flying up and down the river as nightfall approaches, all looking for a safe sandbar on which to spend the night, and with the juvenile birds calling constantly in their parents in the fading light, touches one's soul at so many levels that it is hard not to weep from the utter magic and power of it all. After every such experience I am as emotionally drained as I am after hearing a perfect performance of a Beethoven symphony, or a sacred Bach composition. The word "religion" comes from the Latin word *religio*, meaning a bond between humans and the gods, and in common with the enduring orchestral music, cranes provide that connection perfectly. Often appearing miraculously from incredible heights like celestial seraphim, and sometimes similarly ascending into the sky until they are lost to human view, our Sandhill Cranes are every bit as wondrous as the angels painted on the ceiling of the Sistine Chapel, and one does not have to travel to Italy to appreciate them.

All wonderful and rare things in this world carry a significant price tag; otherwise they would be neither rare nor so highly valued. The price tag on our cranes is simply this: we must be willing to protect from destruction the wonderful river that crosses Nebraska like a beautiful quicksilver necklace, the Platte River. Beyond its rich historic value, the Platte is easily the most valuable and most threatened of our surface waters. It is a river that millions of bison once drank from, and one along which tens of thousands of immigrants once passed on their way to building a complete America. Wading in that graceful river is like wading into history; it is a river that offers many quiet gifts to us. Yet, these are also rich gifts that we must be willing to protect, cherish, and finally to pass on to our children as if they were our collective family's greatest treasures, which in fact they are.

I offered such a gift recently, when for the first time I took my seven-year-old granddaughter to see the Sandhill Cranes on the Platte. She had been asking me to take her for several years: indeed, ever since her mother explained that the cranes I spent so much time watching each year weren't the kind of machinery cranes she already knew about. This year, armed with a pair of binoculars and the knowledge garnered by reading a children's book on cranes, she was finally ready.

This March, like unnumbered Marches before it, the cranes have again returned to the Platte Valley. Their annual predictable appearance is like watching a favorite spring flower unfolding, a piece of music developing, a promise being fulfilled. That promise is being paid annually by the experienced migrant cranes to all the generations of cranes that have stopped in the Platte Valley in eons past. The present generation must instill among the less experienced birds a firm memory of the Platte, the locations of its wet meadows, its abundant grainfields, and a collective memory of its gentle evenings, when the river's cool waters lap at the feet of the cranes as they stand all night in shallow waters around the edges of the Platte's innumerable sandbars and islands.

The sights and sounds of cranes roosting on the Platte are immeasurably old, but are also forever new and variable. Early one March morning, as night slowly gave rise to dawn on the Platte River, the planet Mars was high in the sky, Venus was brilliant in the eastern sky, and the moon was approaching fullness. Great Horned Owls sang occasional duets, and the cranes talked to one another with increasing urgency. Then, just before sunrise, the cranes rose majestically in flock after flock, along with even larger groups of Canada Geese, and headed toward feeding grounds south of the river. To one who has never experienced the visual and aural components of such a scene, it is nearly impossible to try to convey, but standing beside railroad tracks as a speeding locomotive passes by may give some slight idea of the sound and implicit power expressed in the takeoff of ten thousand cranes.

I once described the music of crane calls as perhaps being most like that of angels singing, but on further thought I believe that this is an unfair comparison. Angel choruses, judging from most paintings one sees, seem to be highly age- or sec-biased in favor of young attractive females, whereas the music of crane flocks exhibit all the democratic exuberance imaginable when every bird, regardless of sex and age, is calling simultaneously at full voice regardless of pitch. Crane chorusing can only remind one of the final movement of Beethoven's Ninth Symphony, as chaotically sung by a vast assemblage of tone-deaf but enthusiastic lovers of fine music.

The evening return by the cranes to the river near sunset each day is not so much a sudden explosion as a gradual buildup of tension and beauty, in a manner resembling Ravel's *Bolero*. As the western skies redden the cranes fly up and down the main channel of the river, calling with gradually increasing urgency, evidently trying to make the decision as to where they might most safely spend their night. Sometimes the weak, chirping voice of a yearling crane, seemingly worried about possibly being separated from its parents in the evening confusion, penetrates the general level of crane conversation. The decision to land is finally made by a few adventuresome souls, and the rest of the birds tumble in behind, all calling at the top of their lungs. Watching this incredibly boisterous activity, my granddaughter turned to me and asked, "Grampa, do the cranes do this only on Saturdays?" Gradually, as twilight descends into night, the noise level of roosting flocks dies down. Yet all night long some cranes in every flock remain awake and stand watch while others sleep with their bills tucked under their wings, the latter presumably secure in the knowledge that some of their group are always alert and watching for danger.

These unspoken promises, both daily and annual, that the cranes keep with one another and with the river remind us of our individual promises and personal obligations to ourselves, our kin, and our land. Holding the hand of a small grandchild, as a flock of cranes passes overhead, and telling her that if she is very lucky she might also one day show these same sights to her own grandchild are a powerful lesson in faith, hope, and love. And beauty, touched by love, is somehow transformed into magic.

—Paul Johnsgard
from *Earth, Water, and Sky*

Clear Evening after Rain

THE SUN SINKS TOWARDS THE HORIZON.
The light clouds are blown away.
A rainbow shines on the river.
The last raindrops spatter the rocks.
Cranes and herons soar in the sky.
Fat bears feed along the banks.
I wait here for the west wind
And enjoy the crescent moon.
Shining through misty bamboos.

—Tu Fu

YOU WHO ARE CONSTANTLY ON MY MIND,
And dear to me as the breath of life –
You depart in obedience to the imperial command,
From the cape of Mitsu in Naniwa Bay,
Where in the evening the cranes call to their mates.
You will board a great ship, full-oared,
And sail away past many an island
On the ocean of high white waves.
Then, I, who remain, will see you go,
Making offerings and prayers to the gods.
Come back soon, O friend!

—Kasa Kanamura
from *The Manyosku: One Thousand Poems*
addressed to an envoy departing for China, in spring 733 AD

The Cranes

THE WESTERN WIND HAS BLOWN *but a few days;*
Yet the first leaf already flies from the bough.
On the drying paths I walk in my thin shoes;
In the first cold I have donned my quilted coat.
Through shallow ditches the floods are clearing away;
Through sparse bamboos trickles a slanting light.
In the early dusk, down an alley of green moss,
The garden-boy is leading the cranes home.
Offers homage to the wild crane.

—Bo Ju-yi
written 830 AD
from *Translations from the Chinese*

Cranes Crying in the Marshes

T HE CRANE IS A SACRED bird. Its cries are most clear. ...
I kept two cranes in the bamboo grove surrounding my lute
hall. Sometimes, in a shadowy place, they would dance together,
other times they would fly up and cry in unison. But they would
always wait for the appropriate time: they did not dance unless
there was a cool breeze to shake their feathers, and they did not
cry unless they could look up to the Milky Way as if they saw the
gods. When the time was not propitious they would neither sing
nor dance.

—Robert H. van Gulik
Second half of the introduction from *Shen-chi-pi-pu,*
Ming Dynasty handbook of lute tunes
from *The Lore of the Chinese Lute*

Brolga, the Dancing Girl

B ROLGA WAS THE FAVOURITE of everyone in the tribe, for she was not only the merriest among them, but also their best dancer. The other women were content to beat the ground while the men danced, but Brolga must dance; the dances of her own creation as well as those she had seen. Her fame spread and many came to see her. Some also desired her in marriage, though she always rejected them.

An evil magician, Nonega, was most persistent in his attention, until the old men of the tribe told him that, because of his tribal relationship and his unpleasant personality, they would never allow Brolga to become his wife. "If I can't have her," snarled Nonega, "she'll never belong to anyone else." For already he had planned to change her from a girl into some creature.

One day, when Brolga was dancing by herself on an open plain near her camp, Nonega, chanting incantations from the centre of a whirlpool in which he was travelling, enveloped the girl in a dense cloud of dust. There was no sign of Brolga after the whirlpool had passed, but standing in her place was a tall, graceful bird, moving its wings in the same manner as the young dancer had moved her arms. When they saw the resemblance everyone called out "Brolga! Brolga!" The bird seemed to understand and, moving towards them, bowed and performed even more intricate dances than before.

From that time onward the aborigines have called the bird Brolga, and they tell their children how the beautiful girl was transformed into the equally beautiful grey bird which still dances on the flood plains of northern Australia.

—Ainslie Roberts
from *The Dawn of Time: Australia Aboriginal Myths*

AS THE TIDE FLOWS INTO WAKA BAY,
The cranes, with the lagoons lost in flood,
Go crying towards the reedy shore.

—Yamabe Akahito
from *The Manyosku: One Thousand Poems*
Written on the occasion of the sovereign's journey to
the province of Ki, in the winter 724 AD

The Python and the Heron

A LITTLE MOUSE was sitting on a little rock when a hungry Python came crawling by and saw him.

"Just what I need!" the Python said to himself. "I'll grab a snack along the way."

He opened his maw and lunged at the Mouse. But the Mouse dodged, and the python swallowed the rock instead.

It stuck in his throat. What was to be done?

He crawled to the Heron, whose long bill was like a huge pair of tweezers. "Help me!" he begged, in a half-choked voice.

"What's the matter?" asked the Heron. "It looks to me as though you've stuffed yourself too full again."

"I swallowed a rock instead of a mouse," wheezed the Python, "and it stuck in my throat."

"Shake your head good and hard," said the Heron.

"I've already tried that."

"Try to cough it up."

"I've tried that, too. I've tried everything, and nothing helps."

"Nothing helps?"

"Nothing at all," wheezed the Python.

"That's good," said the Heron.

—Sergei Makhalkov
from *Let's Fight!: And other Russian Fables*

#4 of *The Seven Poems* by *Saigyo Hoshi*

Startled
By a single scream
Of the crane which is reposing
On the surface of the swamp,
All the (other) birds are crying.

Sawa no omi ni
Fuse-taru tazu no
Hito koye ni
Odorokasarete
Chidori naku-nari.

—Saigyo Hoshi
Japanese version translated by Arthur Waley
from *Japanese Poetry, The Uta*
Uta means verse of the thirty-one syllables

The Storks

A STORK HAD BUILT his nest on the roof of the last house in a little town.

The mother stork was sitting on the nest with her little ones, who stuck out their little black beaks, which had not turned red yet. The father stork stood a little way off on the ridge of the roof, erect and stiff, with one leg drawn up under him, so as at least to be at some trouble while standing sentry. One might have thought he was carved out of wood, he stood so still!

"It will look so grand for my wife to have a sentry on guard by the nest!" he thought. "People won't know that I am her husband, I daresay they think I have orders to stand there—it looks smart!" and so he remained standing on one leg.

A party of children were playing in the street, and when they saw the stork, one of the boldest boys, followed by the others, sang the old song about the storks, but he sang it just as it came into his head,

"Oh! father stork, father stork, fly to your nest,
Three featherless fledglings await your return.
The first of your chicks shall be stuck through the breast
The second shall hang and the third shall burn."

Hark! What are the boys singing?" said the little storks. "They say we are to hanged and burnt!"

Don't bother your heads about them!" said the mother stork; "don't listen to them and then it won't do you any harm."

But the boys went on singing and pointing their fingers at the storks; only one boy, whose name was Peter, said that it was a shame to make fun of the creatures and he would take no part in it.

The mother bird comforted her little ones saying, "Do not trouble yourselves about it, look at your father how quietly he stands, and on one leg too!"

"But we are so frightened," said the young ones, burying their heads in the nest.

The next day when the children came back to play and they saw the storks they began their old song,

"The first of your chicks shall be stuck through the breast
The second shall hang and the third shall burn."

"Are we to be hanged and burnt?" asked the little storks.

"No, certainly not!" said the mother; "you are to learn to fly, see if I don't drill you, then we will go into the fields and visit the frogs; they curtsey in the water to us and sing 'Koax, Koax,' and then we gobble them up; that's a treat if you like!"

"And what next?" asked the young ones.

15

"Oh, then all the storks in the country assemble for the autumn maneuvers, and you will have to fly your best, for the one who cannot fly will be run through the body by the general's beak, so you must take good care to learn something when the drills begin."

"After all then we may be staked just as the boys said, and listen, they are singing it again now!"

"Listen to me and not to them," said the mother stork. "After the grand maneuvers we shall fly away to the warm countries, ever such a way off, over the woods and mountains. We go to Egypt where they have three-cornered houses the points of which reach above the clouds; they are called Pyramids, and they are older than any stork can imagine. Then there is a river which overflows its banks and all the land round turns to mud. You walk about in mud devouring frogs."

"Oh!" said all the young ones.

"Yes, it is splendid, you do nothing but eat all day; while we are so well off there, there is not a leaf on the trees in this country, and it is so cold that the clouds freeze all to pieces and fall down in little bits."

She meant snow, but did not know how to describe it any better.

"Do the naughty boys freeze to pieces?" asked the young storks.

"No, they don't freeze to pieces, but they come very near to it and have to sit moping in dark rooms; you, on the other hand, fly about in strange countries, in the warm sunshine among flowers."

Some time passed and the little ones were big enough to stand up in the nest and look about them. The father stork flew backwards and forwards every day, with nice frogs and little snakes, and every kind of delicacy he could find. It was so funny to see the tricks he did to amuse them; he would turn his head right round on to his tail, and he would clatter with his beak, as if it was a rattle. And then he told them all the stories he heard in the swamps.

"Well, now you must learn to fly," said the mother stork one day; and all the young ones had to stand on the ridge of the roof.

Oh, how they wobbled about trying to keep their balance with their wings, and how nearly they fell down.

"Now look at me," said the mother; "this is how you must hold your heads! And move your legs so! One, two, one, two, this will all help you to get on in the world."

Then she flew a little way, and the young ones made a clumsy little hop, and down they came with a bump, for their bodies were too heavy.

"I don't want to fly," said one of the young ones, creeping down into the nest again. "I don't care about going to the warm countries."

"Do you want to freeze to death here when the winter comes? Shall the boys come and hang or burn or stake you? I will soon call them!"

"No, no," said the young one, hopping up on to the roof again, just like the others.

By the third day they could all fly fairly well; then they thought they could hover in the air, too, and they tried it, but flop!—they soon found they had to move their wings again.
Then the boys began their song again:

"Oh! father stork, father stork, fly to your nest."

"Shall we fly down and pick their eyes out?" asked the young ones.

"No, leave them alone," said their mother; "only pay attention to me, that is much more important. One, two, three, now we fly to the right; one, two, three, now to the left, and round the chimney! that was good. That last stroke of the wings was so pretty and the flap so well done that I will allow you to go to the swamp with me tomorrow! Several nice storks go there with their children; now just let me see that mine are the nicest. Don't forget to carry your heads high; it looks well, and gives you an air of importance."

"But are we not to have our revenge on the naughty boys?" asked the young storks.

"Let them scream as much as they like; you will fly away with the clouds to the land of the pyramids, while they will perhaps be freezing. There won't be a green leaf or a sweet apple here then!"

"But we *will* have our revenge!" they whispered to each other, and then they began their drilling again.

Of all the boys in the street, not one was worse at making fun of the storks than he who first began the derisive song. He was a tiny little fellow, not more than six years old. It is true, the young storks thought he was at least a hundred, for he was so much bigger than their father and mother, and they had no idea how old children and grown-up people could be. They reserved all their vengeance for the boy who first began to tease them, and who never would leave off. The young storks were frightfully irritated by the teasing, and the older they grew the less they would stand it. At last their mother was obliged to promise that they should have their revenge, but not till the last day before they left.

"We shall first have to see you behave at the maneuvers! If you come to grief and the general has to run you through the breast with his beak, the boys will after all be right, at least in one way! Now let us see!"

"That you shall!" said the young ones; and didn't they take pains! They practiced every day, till they could fly as lightly as any feather; it was quite a pleasure to watch them.

Then came the autumn; all the storks began to assemble, before they started on their flight to the warm countries, where they spend their winters.

Those were indeed maneuvers! They had to fly over woods and towns, to try their wings, because they had such a long journey before them. The young storks did everything so well, that they got no end of frogs and snakes as prizes. They had the best characters, and then they could eat the frogs and snakes afterwards, which you may be sure they did.

"Now we shall have our revenge!" they said.

"Yes, certainly," said the mother stork. "My plan is this, and I think it is the right one! I know the pond where all the little human babies lie, till the storks fetch them, and give them to their parents. The pretty little creatures lie there asleep, dreaming sweet dreams, sweeter than any they ever dream afterwards. Every parent wishes for such a little baby, and every child wants a baby brother or sister. Now we fly to the pond and fetch a little brother or sister for each of those children who did not join in singing that horrid song, or in making fun of the storks. But those who sang it shall not have one."

"But what about that bad wicked boy who first began the song!" shrieked the young storks; "what is to be done to him?"

"In the pond there is a little dead baby, it has dreamed itself to death, we will take it to him, and then he will cry, because we have brought him a little dead brother. But you have surely not forgotten the good boy, who said 'It is a shame to make fun of the creatures!' We will take both a brother and a sister to him, and because his name is Peter, you shall all be called Peter too."

It happened just as she said, and all the storks are called Peter to this day.

—Hans Christian Andersen

WHEN CRANES DO LEAVE *their summer dwelling, Thrace,*
And change Strymona with the warmer river Nile:
With wings they write plain letters, varying place,
Scribbling in air with quills uncut and wild.
—Claudius Claudianus

From *The Great Summons*

PEACOCKS SHALL FILL YOUR gardens; you shall rear
The rock and phoenix, and red jungle-fowl,
Whose cry at dawn assembles river storks
To join the play of cranes and ibises;
Where the wild-swan all day
Pursues the glint of idle kingfishers.
O Soul, come back to watch the birds in flight!

—Traditionally attributed to Ch'u Yuan
From *Translations from the Chinese*

The Peacock and the Crane

T HE PEACOCK AND the crane having by chance met together, the peacock erected his tail, displayed his gaudy plumes, and looked with contempt upon the crane, as some mean ordinary person. The crane, resolving to mortify his insolence, took occasion to say that peacocks were very fine birds indeed, if fine feathers could make them so; but that he thought it a much nobler thing to be able to rise above the clouds in the endless space, and survey the wonders of the heavens, as well as of the earth beneath, with its seas, lakes, and rivers, as far as the eyes could reach, then strut upon the ground, and be gazed by children.

Moral: There cannot be a greater sign of a weak mind, then a person's valuing himself on a gaudy outside.

—Thomas Bewick
from *The Fables of Aesop and Other with Designs on Wood*

Short Poems on Various Subjects, Two Selections - #2

MORNINGS THE SPARROW TWITTERS SEEKING FOOD
The dove at evening coos to woo her mate.
Only the crane knows its hours
Cries but not for itself.
And the dumb female cicada never cries
What she feels she does not display.
Only the frogs croak with no good reason
Making up a tumult of noise and nuisance.

—Han Yu
from *Sunflower Splendor,*
Three Thousand Years of Chinese Poetry

From *Thoughts in Early Autumn: Thirty Rhymes*

ALL THINGS, LARGE OR SMALL, LIVE IN PEACE.
The road home is flocked by the two Hsiao cliffs.
Follow the prints of cranes on sandbanks,
While honey on the cliffs incites men to lean out too far.
Do not say that river and lakes are eternal.

—Lu Kuei-meng
from *Sunflower Splendor,*
Three Thousand Years of Chinese Poetry

Arap Sang and the Cranes

A gift is a great responsibility to the giver, people of Africa say,
and after they have said that they may tell you the
story of "Arap Sang and the Cranes."

A RAP SANG WAS A GREAT chief and more than half a god, for in the days when he lived great chiefs were always a little mixed up with the gods. One day he was walking on the plain admiring the cattle.

It was hot. The rains had not yet come; the ground was almost bare of grass and hard as stone; the thorn trees gave no shade for they were just made of long spines and thin twigs and tiny leaves and the sun went straight through them.

It was hot. Only the black ants didn't feel it and they would be happy in a furnace.

22

Arap Sang was getting old and the sun beat down on his bald head (he was sensitive about this and didn't like it mentioned) and he thought: "I'm feeling things more than I used to."

And then he came across a vulture sitting in the crotch of a tree, his wings hanging down and his eyes on the outlook.

"Vulture," said Arap Sang, "I'm hot and the sun is making my head ache. You have there a fine pair of broad wings. I'd be most grateful if you'd spread them out and let an old man enjoy a patch of shade."

"Why?" croaked Vulture. He had indigestion. Vultures usually have indigestion; it's the things they eat.

"Why?" said Arap Sang mildly. "Now that's a question to which I'm not certain that I've got the answer. Why? Why, I suppose, because I ask you. Because I'm an old man and entitled to a little assistance and respect. Because it wouldn't be much trouble to you. Because it's pleasant and good to help people."

"Bah!" said Vulture.

"What's that?"

"Oh, go home, Baldy, and stop bothering people; it's hot."

Arap Sang straightened himself up and his eyes flashed. He wasn't half a god for nothing and when he was angry he could be rather a terrible old person. And he was very angry now. It was that remark about his lack of hair.

The really terrifying thing was that when he spoke he didn't shout. He spoke quietly and the words were clear and cold and hard. And all separate like hailstones.

"Vulture," he said, "you're cruel and you're selfish. I shan't forget what you've said and you won't either. NOW GET OUT!"

Arap Sang was so impressive that Vulture got up awkwardly and flapped off.

"Silly old fool," he said uncomfortably.

Presently he met an acquaintance of his (vultures don't have friends, they just have acquaintances) and they perched together on the same bough. Vulture took a close look at his companion and then another and what he saw was so funny that it cheered him up.

"He, he!" he giggled. "What's happened to you? Met with an accident? You're bald."

The other vulture looked sour, but at the same time you felt he might be pleased about something.

"That's good, coming from you," he said. "What have you been up to? You haven't got a feather on you above the shoulders."

Then they both felt their heads with consternation. It was quite true. They were bald, both of them, and so was every other vulture, the whole family, right down to this very day.

Which goes to show that if you can't be ordinarily pleasant to people at least it's not wise to go insulting great chiefs who are half gods.

I said that he was rather a terrible old person.

Arap Sang walked on. He was feeling shaky. Losing his temper always upset him afterward, and doing the sort of magic that makes every vulture in the world bald in the wink of an eye takes it out of you if you aren't as young as you used to be.

And he did want a bit of shade.

Presently he met an elephant. Elephant was panting across the plain in a tearing hurry and was most reluctant to stop when Arap Sang called to him.

"Elephant," said Arap Sang weakly. "I'm tired and I'm dizzy. I want to get to the forest and into a bit of shade but it's a long way."

"It is hot, isn't it?" said Elephant. I'm off to the forest myself."

Would you spread out your great ears and let me walk along under them?" asked Arap Sang.

"I'm sorry," said Elephant, "but you'd make my journey so slow. I must get to the forest. I've got the most terrible headache."

"Well, I've got a headache too," protested the old man.

"I'm sure," said Elephant, " and no one could be sorrier about that than I am. Is it a very big headache?"

"Shocking big," said Arap Sang.

"There now," said Elephant. "Consider how big I am compared to you and what the size of my headache must be."

That's elephants all over, always so logical. Arap Sang felt that there was something wrong with this argument but he couldn't just see where. Also he had become a little uncomfortable about all those bald vultures and he didn't want to lose his temper with anyone else. You have to be careful what you do when you're half a god. It's so dreadfully final.

Oh, all right," he muttered.

"Knew you'd see it that way," said Elephant. "It's just what I was saying about you the other day. You can always rely on Arap Sang, I said, to behave reasonably. Well, goodbye and good luck."

And he hurried off in the direction of the distant forest and was soon out of sight.

Poor Arap Sang was now feeling very ill indeed. He sat on the ground and he thought to himself: "I can't go another step unless I get some shade and if I don't get some soon I'm done for."

And there he was found by a flock of cranes.

They came dancing through the white grass, stamping their long delicate legs so that the insects flew up in alarm and were at once snapped up in the cranes' beaks. They gathered round Arap

Sang sitting on the ground and he looked so old and distressed that they hopped up and down with embarrassment, first on one leg then the other. "Korong! Korong!" they called softly and this happens to be their name as well.

"Good birds," whispered Arap Sang, "you must help me. If I don't reach shade soon I'll die. Help me to the forest."

"But, of course," said the cranes, and they spread their great handsome black and white wings to shade him and helped him to his feet, and together, slowly, they all crossed the plain into the trees.

Then Arap Sang sat in the shade of a fine cotton tree and felt very much better. The birds gathered round him and he looked at them and thought that he had never seen more beautiful creatures in the whole world.

"And kind. Kind as well as beautiful," he muttered. "The two don't always go together. I must reward them."

I shan't forget your kindness," he said, "and I'll see that no one else does. Now I want each of you to come here."

Then the cranes came one after another and bowed before him and Arap Sang stretched out his kindly old hand and gently touched each beautiful sleek head. And where he did this a golden crown appeared and after the birds had gravely bowed their thanks they all flew off to the lake, their new crowns glittering in the evening sun.

Arap Sang felt quite recovered. He was very pleased with his gift to the cranes.

Two months later a crane dragged himself to the door of Arap Sang's house. It was a pitiful sight, thin with hunger, feathers broken and muddy from hiding in the reeds, eyes red with lack of sleep.

Arap Sang exclaimed in pity and horror.

"Great Chief," said the crane, "we beg you to take back your gift. If you don't there'll soon be not one crane left alive for we are hunted day and night for the sake of our golden crowns."

Arap Sang listened and nodded his head in sorrow.

"I'm old and I'm foolish," he said, "and I harm my friends. I had forgotten that men also were greedy and selfish and they'll do anything for gold. Let me undo the wrong I have done by giving without thought. I'll make one more magic but that'll be the last."

Then he took their golden crowns and in their place he put a wonderful halo of feathers which they have until this day.

But they still are called Crowned Cranes.

—Humphrey Harman
abbreviated from *Tales Told near a Crocodile: Stories from Nyanza*
Nyanza is a province in Kenya, Central Africa,
on the northern shores of Lake Victoria.

The Parliament of Fowls

This poetry in "The Parliament of Fowls" tells of the mating of fowls on St. Valentine's Day and is thought to celebrate the betrothal of Richard II to Anne of Boliemia.

...There was the dove, with her eyes meek
The jealous swan, ayens his death that singeth,
The owl eke, that of death the bode brigheth.
The crane, the giant, with his trumpet sound;
The thief, the chough, and eke the jangling pye;
The scorning jay; the eel's foe, the heron,
The false lapwing, full of treachery...

The Parlement of Foules *(original form)*
...Ther was the douve, with hir eyen meke;
The Ialous swan, ayens his deth that singeth;
The oule eek, that of dethe the bode bringeth;
The crane the geaunt, with his trompes soune;
The theef, the chogh; and eek the Iangling pye;
The scorning Iay; the eles foo, the heroune;
The false lapwing, ful of trecherye...

—Geoffrey Chaucer
from *The Works of Geoffrey Chaucer*
with permission of Oxford University Press

Hidden in the Blind

SO STILL THAT BEWITCHING TRESPASS;
to lie low and poach
upon the private lives
of families
in their most intimate hour.

To hear crouched
the contented chuk and squabble
from the sandbar
as light to purple
lowers wings
upon the cold March night.

To stare shamelessly
at the couples dancing adagio
across the lawn
to music lifting
from ten thousand cranes,
bearing witness to a spy
that there are no secrets.
—Anne Meredith McCollister

RIPPLING RIVER FLOWS
Winding past my river home——
Sleepy frog sits near.
Long-legged crane creeps in closer,
Rippling river flows on, on——
untitled tanka by Cheryl J. Wilkinson

The Marsh King's Daughter

THE STORKS HAVE A GREAT many stories, which they tell their little ones, all about the bogs and the marshes. They suit them to their ages and capacity. The youngest ones are quite satisfied with "Kribble krabble," or some such nonsense; but the older ones want something with more meaning in it, or at any rate something about the family. We all know one of the two oldest and longest tales which have been kept up among the storks; the one about Moses, who was placed by his mother on the waters of the Nile, and found there by the king's daughter. How she brought him up and how he became a great man whose burial place nobody to this day knows. This is all common knowledge.

The other story is not known yet, because the storks have kept it among themselves. It has been handed on from one mother stork to another for more than a thousand years, and each succeeding mother has told it better and better, till we now tell it best of all.

The first pair of storks who told it, and who actually lived it, had their summer quarters on the roof of the Viking's timbered house up by "Vidmosen" (the Wild Bog) in Wendsyssel. It is in the county of Hiorring, high up toward the Skaw, in the north of Jutland, if we are to describe it according to the authorities. There is still a great bog there, which we may read about in the county chronicles. This district used to be under the sea at one time but the ground has risen, and it stretches for miles. It is surrounded on every side by marshy meadows, quagmires, and peat bogs, on which grow cloud berries and stunted bushes. There is nearly always a damp mist hanging over it, and seventy years ago it was still overrun with wolves. It may well be called the Wild Bog, and one can easily imagine how desolate and dreary it was among all these swamps and pools a thousand years ago. In detail everything is much the same now as it was then. The reeds grow to the same height, and have the same kind of long purple-brown leaves with feathery tips as now. The birch still grows there with its white bark and its delicate loosely hanging leaves. With regard to living creatures, the flies still wear their gauzy draperies of the same cut; and the storks now, as then, still dress in black and white, with long red stockings. The people certainly then had a very different cut for their clothes than at the present day; but if any of them, serf or huntsman, or anybody at all, stepped on the quagmires, the same fate befell him a thousand years ago as would overtake him now if he ventured on them—in he would go, and down he would sink to the Marsh King, as they call him. He rules down below over the whole kingdom of bogs and swamps. He might also be called King of the Quagmires, but we prefer to call him the Marsh King, as the storks did. We know very little about his rule, but that is perhaps just as well.

Near the bogs, close to the arm of the Cattegat, called the Limfiord, lay the timbered hall of the Vikings with its stone cellar, its tower and its three storys. The storks had built their nest on the top of the roof, and the mother stork was sitting on the eggs which she was quite sure would soon be successfully hatched.

One evening Father stork stayed out rather late, and when he came back he looked somewhat ruffled.

"I have something terrible to tell you!" he said to the mother stork.

"Don't tell it to me then," she answered; "remember that I am sitting, it might upset me and that would be bad for the eggs!"

"You will have to know it," said he; "she has come here, the daughter of our host in Egypt. She has ventured to take the journey, and now she has disappeared."

"She who is related to the fairies! Tell me all about it. You know I can't bear to be kept waiting now I am sitting."

"Look here, Mother! She must have believed what the doctor said as you told me; she believed that the marsh flowers up here would do something for her father, and she flew over here in feather plumage with the other two princesses, who have to come north every year to take the baths to make themselves young. She came, and she has vanished."

"You go into too many particulars," said the mother stork; "the eggs might get a chill, and I can't stand being kept in suspense."

"I have been on the outlook," said Father stork, "and tonight when I was among the reeds where the quagmire will hardly bear me, I saw three swans flying along, and there was something about their flight which said to me, 'Watch them, they are not real swans! They are only in swan's plumage.' You know, Mother, as well as I, that one feels things intuitively, whether or not they are what they seem to be."

"Yes, indeed!" she said, "but tell me about the princess, I am quite tired of hearing about swan's plumage."

"You know that in the middle of the bog there is a kind of lake," said Father stork. "You can see a bit of it if you raise your head. Well, there was a big alder stump between the bushes and the quagmire, and on this the three swans settled, flapping their wings and looking about them. Then one of them threw off the swan's plumage, and I at once recognized in her our princess from Egypt. There she sat with no covering but her long black hair; I heard her beg the two others to take good care of the swan's plumage while she dived under the water to pick up the marsh flower which she thought she could see. They nodded and raised their heads, and lifted up the loose plumage. What are they going to do with it, thought I, and she no doubt asked them the same thing; and the answer came, she had ocular demonstration of it: they flew up into the air with the feather garment! 'Just you duck down,' they cried. "Never again will you fly about in the guise of a swan; nevermore will you see the land of Egypt; you may sit in your swamp.' Then they tore the feather garment into a hundred bits, scattering the feathers all over the place, like a snowstorm; then away flew those two good-for-nothing princesses."

"What a terrible thing," said Mother stork; "but I must have the end of it."

"The princess moaned and wept! Her tears trickled down upon the alder stump, and then it began to move, for it was the Marsh King himself, who lives in the bog. I saw the stump turn round, and saw that it was no longer a stump; it stretched out long miry branches like arms. The poor child was terrified, and she sprang away on to the shaking quagmire where it would not even bear my weight, far less hers. She sank at once and the alder stump after her, it was dragging her down. Great black bubbles rose in the slime, and then there was nothing more to be seen. Now she is buried in the Wild Bog and never will she take back the flowers she came for to Egypt. You could not have endured the sight, Mother!"

"You shouldn't even tell me anything of the sort just now, it might have a bad effect upon the eggs. The princess must look after herself! She will get help somehow; if it had been you or I now, or one of our sort, all would have been over with us!"

"I mean to keep a watch though, every day," said the stork, and he kept his word.

But a long time passed, and then one day he saw that a green stem shot up from the fathomless depths, and when it reached the surface of the water, a leaf appeared at the top which grew broader and broader. Next a bud appeared close by it and one morning at dawn, just as the stork was passing, the bud opened out in the warm rays of the sun, and in the middle of it lay a lovely baby, a little girl, looking just as fresh as if she had just come out of a bath. She was so exactly like the princess from Egypt that at first the stork thought it was she who had grown small; but when he put two and two together, he came to the conclusion that it was her child and the Marsh King's. This explained why she appeared in a water lily. "She can't stay there very long," thought the stork; "and there are too many of us in my nest as it is, but an idea has just come into my head! The Viking's wife has no child, and she has often wished for one. As I am always said to bring the babies, this time I will do so in earnest. I will fly away to the Viking's wife with the baby, and that will indeed be a joy for her."

So the stork took up the little girl and flew away with her to the timbered house where he picked a hole in the bladder skin which covered the window, and laid the baby in the arms of the Viking's wife. This done he flew home and told the mother stork all about it; and the young ones heard what he said, they were old enough to understand it.

"So you see that the princess is not dead; she must have sent the baby up here and I have found a home for her."

"I said so from the very first," said Mother stork; "now just give a little attention to your own children, it is almost time to start on our own journey. I feel a tingling in my wings every now and then! The cuckoo and the nightingale are already gone, and I hear from the quails that we shall soon have a good wind. Our young people will do themselves credit at the maneuvers if I know them aright.

How delighted the Viking's wife was when she woke in the morning and found the little baby on her bosom. She kissed and caressed it; but it screamed and kicked terribly, and seemed anything but happy. At last it cried itself to sleep, and as it lay there a prettier little thing could not have been seen. The Viking's wife was delighted, body and soul were filled with joy. She was sure that now her husband and all his men would soon come back as unexpectedly as the baby had come. So she and her household busied themselves in putting the house in order against their return. The long colored tapestries which she and her handmaids had woven with pictures of their gods—Odin, Thor and Freya as they were called—were hung up. The serfs had to scour and polish the old shields which hung round the walls; cushions were laid on the benches, and logs upon the great hearth in the middle of the hall, so that the fire might be lighted at once. The Viking's wife helped with all this work herself so that when evening came she was very tired and slept soundly.

When she woke toward morning she was much alarmed at finding that the little baby had disappeared. She sprang up and lighted a pine chip and looked about. There was no baby, but at the foot of the bed sat a hideous toad. She was horrified at the sight, and seized up a heavy stick to kill it, but it looked at her with such curious sad eyes, that she had not the heart to strike it. Once more she looked round and the toad gave a faint pitiful croak which made her start. She jumped out of bed and threw open the window shutter, the sun was just rising and its beams fell upon the bed and the great toad. All at once the monster's wide mouth seemed to contract, and to become small and rosy, the limbs stretched and again took their lovely shapes, and it was her own dear little baby which lay there, and not a hideous frog.

"Whatever is this?" she cried. "I have had a bad dream. This is my own darling elfin child." She kissed it and pressed it to her heart, but it struggled and bit like a wild kitten.

Neither that day nor the next did the Viking lord come home although he was on his way, but the winds were against him; they were blowing southward for the storks. "It is an ill wind that blows nobody good."

In the course of a few days and nights it became clear to the Viking's wife how matters stood with her little baby; some magic power had a terrible hold over her. In the daytime it was as beautiful as any fairy, but it had a bad, wicked temper; at night on the other hand she became a hideous toad, quiet and pathetic with sad mournful eyes. There were two natures in her both in soul and body continually shifting. The reason of it was that the little girl brought by the frog, by day had her mother's form and her father's evil nature; but at night her kinship with him appeared in her outward form, and her mother's sweet nature and gentle spirit beamed out of the misshapen monster. Who could release her from the power of this witchcraft? It caused the Viking's wife much grief and trouble, and yet her heart yearned over the unfortunate being. She knew that she would never dare to tell her husband the true state of affairs, because he would without doubt, according to custom, have the poor child exposed on the highway for anyone who chose to look after it. The good woman had not the heart to do this, and so she determined that he should only see the child by broad daylight.

One morning there was a sound of stork's wings swishing over the roof; during the night more than a hundred pairs of storks had made it their resting place, after the great maneuvers, and they were now trying their wings before starting on their long southward flight.

"Every man ready!" they cried; "all the wives and children too."

"How light we feel," cried the young storks; "our legs tingle as if we were full of live frogs! How splendid it is to be traveling to foreign lands."

"Keep in line!" said Father and Mother, "and don't let your beaks clatter so fast, it isn't good for the chest." Then away they flew.

At the very same moment a horn sounded over the heath. The Viking had landed with all his men; they were bringing home no end of rich booty from the Gallic coast, where the people cried in their terror as did the people of Britain:

"Deliver us from the wild Northmen!"

What life and noise came to the Viking's home by the Wild Bog now. The mead cask was brought into the hall, the great fire lighted, and horses slaughtered for the feast, which was to be an uproarious one. The priest sprinkled the thralls with the warm blood of the horses as a consecration. The fire crackled and roared, driving the smoke up under the roof, and the soot dripped down from the beams; but they were used to all that. Guests were invited and they received handsome presents. All feuds and double dealing were forgotten. They drank deeply, and threw the knucklebones in each other's faces when they had gnawed them, but that was a mark of good feeling. The skald— the minstrel of the times, but he was also a warrior, for he went with them on their expeditions, and he knew what he was singing about—gave them one of his ballads recounting all their warlike deeds and their prowess. After every verse came the same refrain: "Fortunes may be lost, friends may die, one dies oneself, but a glorious name never dies!" Then they banged on the shields, and hammered with knives or the knucklebones on the table before them, till the hall rang.

The Viking's wife sat on the cross bench in the banqueting hall. She was dressed in silk with gold bracelets and large amber beads. The skald brought her name into the song too; he spoke of the golden treasure she had brought to her wealthy husband, and his delight at the beautiful child which at present he had only seen under its charming daylight guise. He rather admired her passionate nature, and said she would grow into a doughty shield maiden or Valkyrie, able to hold her own in battle. She would be of the kind who would not blink if a practised hand cut off her eyebrows in jest with a sharp sword. The barrel of mead came to an end, and a new one was rolled up in its place; this one too was soon drained to the dregs, but they were a hardheaded people who could stand a great deal. They had a proverb then, "the beast knows when it is time to go home from grass, but the fool never knows when he has had enough." They knew it very well, but people often know one thing and yet do another. They also knew that "the dearest friend becomes a bore if he sits too long in one's house!" but yet they sat on. Meat and drink are such good things! They were a jovial company! At night the thralls slept among the warm ashes, and they dipped their fingers in the sooty grease and licked them. Those were rare times indeed.

The Viking went out once more that year on a raid although the autumn winds were beginning; he sailed with his men to the cost of Britain, "it was just over the water," he said. His wife remained at home with the little girl, and certain it was that the foster-mother soon grew fonder of the poor toad with the pathetic eyes, and plaintive sighs, than she was of the little beauty who tore and bit.

The raw, wet autumn fog "gnaw-worn" which gnaws the leaves off the trees, lay over wood and heath; and "bird loose-feather," as they call the snow, followed closely upon each other. Winter was on its way. The sparrows took the storks' nest under their protection, and discussed the absent owners in their own fashion. The stork couple and their young—where were they now?

The storks were in the land of Egypt under such a sun as we have on a warm summer's day! They were surrounded by flowering tamarinds and acacias. Mahomet's crescent glittered from every cupola on the mosques, and many a pair of storks stood on the slender towers resting after their long journey. Whole flocks of them had their nests side by side on the mighty pillars, or the ruined arches of the deserted temples. The date palm lifted high its screen of branches as if to form a sunshade. The grayish white pyramids stood like shadowy sketches against the clear atmosphere of the desert where the ostrich knew it would find space for its stride. The lion crouched gazing with its great wise eyes at the marble Sphinx half buried in the sand. The Nile waters had receded and the land teemed with frogs; to the storks this was the most splendid sight in all the land. The eyes of the young ones were quite dazzled with the sight.

"See what it is to be here, and we always have the same in our warm country," said the mother stork, and the stomachs of the little ones tingled.

"Is there anything more to see?" they asked. "Shall we go any farther inland?"

"There is not much more to see," said the mother stork. "On the fertile side there are only secluded woods where the trees are interlaced by creeping plants. The elephant, with its strong clumsy legs, is the only creature which can force a way through. The snakes there are too big for us, and the lizards are too nimble. If you go out into the desert you will get sand in your eyes if the weather is good, and if it is bad you may be buried in a sandstorm. No, we are best here; there are plenty of frogs and grasshoppers. Here I stay and you too!" And so she stayed.

The old ones stayed in their nests on the slender minarets resting themselves, but at the same time busily smoothing their feathers and rubbing their beaks upon their red stockings. Or they would lift up their long necks and gravely bow their heads, their brown eyes beaming wisely. The young stork misses walked about gravely among the juicy reeds, casting glances at the young bachelor storks, or making acquaintance with them; they would swallow a frog at every third step, or walk about with a small snake dangling from their beak, it had such a good effect they thought, and then it tasted so good. The young he-storks engaged in many a petty quarrel, in which they flapped their wings furiously and stabbed each other with their beaks till the blood came. Then they took mates and built nests for themselves; it was what they lived for. New quarrels soon arose, for in these warm countries people are terribly passionate. All the same it was very pleasant to the old ones, nothing could be wrong that their young ones did. There was sunshine every day, and plenty to eat; nothing to think of but pleasure!

But in the great palace of their Egyptian host, as they called him, matters were not so pleasant. The rich and mighty lord lay stretched upon his couch, as stiff in every limb as if he had been a mummy. The great painted hall was as gorgeous as if he had been lying within a tulip. Relatives and friends stood around him—he was not dead—yet he could hardly be called living. The healing marsh flower from the northern lands, which was to be found and plucked by the one who loved him best, would never be brought. His young and lovely daughter, who in the plumage of a swan had flown over sea and land to the far north, would never return. The two other swan princesses had come back and this is the tale they told:

"We were all flying high up in the air when a huntsman saw us and shot his arrow; it pierced our young friend to the heart and she slowly sank. As she sank she sang her farewell song and fell into the midst of a forest pool. There by the shore under a drooping birch we buried her; but we had our revenge; we bound fire under the wings of a swallow which had its nest under the eaves of his cottage. The roof took fire and the cottage blazed up and he was burnt in it. The flames shone on the pool where she lay, earth of the earth, under the birch. Nevermore will she come back to the land of Egypt."

Then they both wept, and the father stork who heard it clattered with his beak and said, "Pack of lies; I should like to drive my beak right into their breasts!"

"Where it would break off, and a nice sight you would be then," said the mother stork. "Think of yourself first and then of your family, everything else comes second to that!"

"I will perch upon the open cupola tomorrow when all the wise and learned folk assemble to talk about the sick man, perhaps they will get a little nearer to the truth!"

The sages met together and talked long and learnedly, but the stork could neither make head nor tail of it. Nothing came of it, however, either for the sick man or for his daughter who was buried in the Wild Bog; but we may just as well hear what they said and we may, perhaps, understand the story better, or at least as well as the stork.

"Love is the food of life! The highest love nourishes the highest life! Only through love can this life be won back!" This had been said and well said, declared the sages.

"It is a beautiful idea!" said Father stork at once.

"I don't rightly understand it," said the mother stork; "however that is not my fault, but the fault of the idea. It really does not matter to me though, I have other things to think about!"

The sages had talked a great deal about love, the difference between the love of lovers, and that of parent and child, light and vegetation and how the sunbeams kissed the mire and forthwith young shoots sprang into being. The whole discourse was so learned that the father stork could not take it in, far less repeat it. He became quite pensive and stood on one leg for a whole day with his eyes half shut. Learning was a heavy burden to him.

Yet one thing the stork had thoroughly comprehended; he had heard from high and low alike what a misfortune it was to thousands of people and to the whole country, that this man should be lying sick without hope of recovery. It would indeed be a blessed day which should see his health restored. "But where blossoms the flower of healing for him?" they had asked of one another, and they had also consulted all their learned writings, the twinkling stars, the winds and the waves. The only answer that the sages had been able to give was, "Love is the food of life!" but how to apply the saying they knew not. At last all were agreed that succor must come through the princess who loved her father with her whole heart and soul. And they at last decided what she was to do. It was more than a year and a day since they had sent her at night, when there was a new moon, out into the desert to the Sphinx. Here she had to push away the sand from the door at the base of it, and walk through the long passage which led right into the middle of the pyramid, where one of the mightiest of their ancient kings lay swathed in his mummy's bands in the midst of his wealth and glory. Here she was to bend her head to the corpse, and it would be revealed to her where she would find healing and salvation for her father.

All this she had done, and the exact spot had been shown her in dreams where in the depths of the morass she would find the lotus flower that would touch her bosom beneath the water. And this she was to bring home. So she flew away in her swan's plumage to the Wild Bog in the far north.

Now all this the father and mother stork had known from the beginning, and they understand the matter better than we did. We know that the Marsh King dragged her down to himself, and that to those at home she was dead and gone. The wisest of them said like the mother stork, "she will look out for herself!" so they awaited her return, not knowing in fact what else to do.

"I think I will snatch away the swans' plumage from the two deceitful princesses," said the father stork. "Then they could not go to the Wild Bog to do any more mischief. I will keep the plumages up there till we find a use for them."

"Up where will you keep them?" asked the mother stork.

"In our nest at the Wild Bog," said he. "The young ones and I can carry them between us, and if they are too cumbersome, there are places enough on the way where we can hide them till our next flight. One plumage would be enough for her, but two are better; it is a good plan to have plenty of wraps in a northern country!"

"You will get no thanks for it," said the mother stork; "but you are the master. I have nothing to say except when I am sitting."

In the meantime the little child in the Viking's hall by the Wild Bog, whither the storks flew in the spring, had a name given her: it was Helga, but such a name was far too gentle for such a wild spirit as dwelt within her. Month by month it showed itself more, and year by year whilst the storks took the same journey, in autumn toward the Nile, and in spring toward the Wild Bog. The little child grew to be a big girl, and before one knew how, she was the loveliest maiden possible of sixteen. The husk was lovely, but the kernel was hard and rough; wilder than most, even in those hard, wild times.

Her greatest pleasure was to dabble her white hands in the blood of the horses slaughtered for sacrifice; in her wild freaks she would bite the heads off the black cocks which the priest was about to slay, and she said in full earnest to her foster father, "If thy foe were to come and throw a rope round the beams of thy house and pull it about thine ears, I would not wake thee if I could. I should not hear him for the tingling of the blood in the ear thou once boxed years ago! I do not forget!"

But the Viking did not believe what she said. He, like everybody else, was infatuated by her beauty, nor did he know how body and soul changed places in his little Helga in the dark hours of the night. She rode a horse bareback as if she were a part of it, nor did she jump off while her steed bit and fought with the other wild horses. She would often throw herself from the cliff into the sea in all her clothes, and swim out to meet the Viking when his boat neared the shore; and she cut off the longest strand of her beautiful long hair to string her bow. "Self made is well made," said she.

The Viking's wife, though strong-willed and strong minded after the fashion of the times, became toward her daughter like any other weak, anxious mother, because she knew that a spell rested over the terrible child. Often when her mother stepped out on to the balcony Helga, from pure love of teasing, it seemed, would sit down upon the edge of the well, throw up her hands and feet, and go backwards plump into the dark narrow hole. Here with her frog's nature she would rise again and clamber out like a cat dripping with water, carrying a perfect stream into the banquet hall, washing aside the green twigs strewn on the floor.

One bond, however, always held little Helga in check, and that was twilight; when it drew near, she became quiet and pensive, allowing herself to be called and directed. An inner perception as it were drew her toward her mother, and when the sun sank and the transformation took place, she sat sad and quiet, shriveled up into the form of a toad. Her body was now much bigger than those creatures ever are, but for that reason all the more unsightly. She looked like a stretched dwarf with the head of a frog and webbed fingers. There was something so piteous in her eyes; and voice she had none, only a hollow croak like the smothered sobs of a dreaming child. Then the Viking's wife would take it on her knee, and looking into its eyes would forget the misshapen form, and would often say, "I could almost wish that thou wouldst always remain my dumb frog child. Thou art more terrible to look at when thou art clothed in beauty." Then she would write runes against sickness and sorcery, and throw them over the miserable girl, but they did no good at all.

"One would never think that she had been small enough to lie in a water lily!" said the father stork. "Now she is grown up, and the very image of her Egyptian mother, whom we never saw again! She did not manage to take such good care of herself as you and the sages said she would. I have been flying across the marsh year in, year out, and never have I seen a trace of her. Yes, I may as well tell you that all these years when I have come on in advance of you to look after the nest and set it to rights, I have spent many a night flying about like an owl or a bat scanning the open water, but all to no purpose. Nor have we had any use for the two swan plumages which the young ones and I dragged up here with so much difficulty; it took us three journeys to get them here. They have lain for years in the bottom of the nest, and if ever a disaster happens, such as a fire in the timbered house, they will be entirely lost."

"And our good nest would be lost too," said the mother stork; "but you think less of that than you do of your feather dresses, and your marsh princess. You had better go down to her one day and stay in the mire for good. You are a bad father to your own chicks and I have always said so since the first time I hatched a brood. If only we or the young ones don't get an arrow through our wings from that mad Viking girl. She doesn't know what she is about. We are rather more at home here than she is, and she ought to remember that. We never forget our obligations. Every year we pay our toll of a feather, an egg, and a young one, as it is only right we should. Do you think that while she is about I care to go down there as I used to do, and as I do in Egypt when I am 'hail fellow well met' with everybody, and where I peep into their pots and kettles if I like? No, indeed; I sit up here vexing myself about her, the vixen, and you too. You should have left her in the water lily, and there would have been an end of her."

"You are much more estimable than your words," said the father stork. "I know you better than you know yourself, my dear." Then he gave a hop and flapped his wings thrice, proudly stretched out his neck and soared away without moving his outspread wings. When he had gone some distance he made some more powerful strokes, his head and neck bending proudly forward, while his plumage gleamed in the sunshine. What strength and speed there were in his flight!

"He is the handsomest of them all yet," said the mother stork; "but I don't tell him that."

The Viking came home early that autumn with his booty and prisoners; among these was a young Christian priest, one of those men who persecuted the heathen gods of the north. There had often been discussions of late, both in the hall and in the women's bower, about the new faith which was spreading in all the countries to the south. Through the holy Ansgarius it had spread as far as Hedeby on the Schlei. Even little Helga had heard of the belief in the "White Christ," who from love to man had given Himself for their salvation. As far as Helga was concerned it had all gone in at one ear and out at the other, as one says. The very meaning of the word "love" only seemed to dawn upon her when she was shriveled up into the form of a frog in her secret chamber, but the Viking's wife had listened to the story and had felt herself strangely moved by these tales about the Son of the only true God.

The men on their return from their raids told them all about the temples built of costly polished stone, which were raised to Him whose message was Love. Once a couple of heavy golden vessels of cunning workmanship were brought home about which hung a peculiar spicy odor. They were censers used by the Christian priests to swing before the altars on which blood never flowed, but where the bread and wine were changed to the Body and Blood of Him who gave Himself for the yet unborn generations.

The young priest was imprisoned in the deep stone cellars of the timber house and his feet and hands were bound with strips of bark. He was as "beautiful as Baldur," said the Viking's wife, and she felt pity for him, but young Helga proposed that he should be hamstrung and be tied to the tails of wild oxen.

"Then would I let the dogs loose on him. Hie and away over marshes and pools; that would be a merry sight, and merrier still would it be to follow in his course."

However, this was not the death the Viking wished him to die, but rather that as a denier and a persecutor of the great gods, he should be offered up in the morning upon the bloodstone in the groves. For the first time a man was to be sacrificed here. Young Helga begged that she might sprinkle the effigies of the gods and the people with his blood. She polished her sharp knife, and when one of the great ferocious dogs, of which there were so many about the place, sprang towards her, she dug her knife into its side, "to try it," she said; but the Viking's wife looked sadly at the wild, badly-disposed girl. When the night came and girl's beauty of body and soul changed places, she spoke tender words of grief from her sorrowful heart. The ugly toad with its ungainly body stood fixing its sad brown eyes upon her, listening and seeming to understand with the mind of a human being.

"Never once to my husband has a word of my double grief through you passed my lips," said the Viking's wife. "My heart is full of grief for you, great is a mother's love! But love never entered your heart, it is like a lump of cold clay. How ever did you get into my house?"

Then the ungainly creature trembled, as if the words touched some invisible chord between body and soul, and great tears came into its eyes.

"A bitter time will come to you," said the Viking's wife, "and it will be a terrible one to me too! Better would it have been, if as a child you had been exposed on the highway, and lulled by the cold to the sleep of death!" And the Viking's wife shed bitter tears, and went away in anger and sorrow, passing under the curtain of skins which hung from the beams and divided the hall.

The shriveled up toad crouched in the corner, and a dead silence reigned. At intervals a half stifled sigh rose within her; it was as if in anguish something came to life in her heart. She took a step forward and listened, then she stepped forward again and grasped the heavy bar of the door with her clumsy hands. Softly she drew it back, and silently lifted the latch, then she took up the lamp which stood in the ante-room. It seemed as if a strong power gave her strength. She drew out the iron bolt from the barred cellar door, and slipped in to the prisoner. He was asleep, she touched him with her cold clammy hand, and when he woke and saw the hideous creature, he shuddered as if he beheld an evil apparition. She drew out her knife and cut his bonds asunder, and then beckoned him to follow her. He named the Holy Name and made the sign of the cross, and as the form remained unchanged, he repeated the words of the Psalmist: "Blessed is the man who hath pity on the poor and needy; the Lord will deliver him in the time of trouble!" Then he asked, "Who art thou, whose outward appearance is that of an animal, whilst thou willingly performest deeds of mercy?"

The toad only beckoned him and led him behind the sheltering curtains down a long passage to the stable, pointed to a horse, on to which he sprang and she after him. She sat in front of him clutching the mane of the animal. The prisoner understood her and they rode at a quick pace along a path he never would have found to the heath. He forgot her hideous form, knowing that the mercy of the Lord worked through the spirits of darkness. He prayed and sang holy songs which made her tremble. Was it the power of prayer and his singing working upon her, or was it the chill air of the advancing dawn? What were her feelings? She raised herself and wanted to stop and jump off the horse, but the

Christian priest held her tightly, with all his strength, and sang aloud a psalm as if this could lift the spell which held her.

The horse bounded on more wildly than before, the sky grew red, and the first sunbeams pierced the clouds. As the stream of light touched her, the transformation took place. She was once more a lovely maiden but her demoniac spirit was the same. The priest held a blooming maiden in his arms and he was terrified at the sight. He stopped the horse and sprang down, thinking he had met with a new device of the evil one. But young Helga sprang to the ground too. The short child's frock only reached to her knee. She tore the sharp knife from her belt and rushed upon the startled man. "Let me get at thee!" she cried, "let me reach thee and my knife shall pierce thee! Thou art ashen pale, beardless slave!"

She closed upon him and they wrestled together, but an invisible power seemed to give strength to the Christian; he held her tight, and the old oak under which they stood seemed to help him, for the loosened roots above the ground tripped her up. Close by rose a bubbling spring and he sprinkled her with water and commanded the unclean spirit to leave her, making the sign of the cross over her according to Christian usage. But the baptismal water has no power if the spring of faith flows not from within. Yet even here something more than man's strength opposed itself, through him, against the evil which struggled within her. Her arms fell, and she looked with astonishment and paling cheeks at this man who seemed to be a mighty magician skilled in secret arts. These were dark runes he was repeating and cabalistic signs he was tracing in the air. She would not have blenched had he flourished a shining sword, or a sharp ax before her face, but she trembled now as he traced the sign of the cross upon her forehead and bosom, and sat before him with drooping head like a wild bird tamed.

He spoke gently to her about the deed of love she had performed for him this night, when she came in the hideous shape of a toad, cut his bonds asunder, and led him out to light and life. She herself was bound, he said, and with stronger bonds than his; but she also, through him, should reach to light and life everlasting. He would take her to Hedeby, to the holy Ansgarius, and there, in that Christian city, the spell would be removed; but she must no longer sit in front of him on the horse, even if she went of her own free will; he dared not carry her thus.

"Thou must sit behind me, not before me; thy magic beauty has a power given by the Evil One which I dread; yet shall I have the victory through Christ!"

He knelt down and prayed humbly and earnestly. It seemed as if the quiet wood became a holy church consecrated by his worship. The birds began to sing as if they too were also of this new congregation, and the fragrance of the wild flowers was as the ambrosial perfume of incense, while the young priest recited the words of Holy Writ: "The Day-spring from on high hath visited us. To give light to them that sit in darkness, and in the shadow of death, to guide their feet into the way of peace."

He spoke of the yearning of all nature for redemption, and while he spoke the horse which had carried them stood quietly by, only rustling among the bramble-bushes, making the ripe, juicy fruit fall into little Helga's hands, as if inviting her to refresh herself. Patiently she allowed herself to be lifted on to the horse's back, and sat there like one in a trance, who neither watches nor wanders. The Christian man bound together two branches in the shape of a cross, which he held aloft in his hand as he rode through the wood. The brushwood grew thicker and thicker, till at last it became a trackless wilderness. Bushes of the wild sloe blocked the way, and they had to ride round them. The bubbling springs turned to standing pools, and these they also had to ride round; still they found strength and refreshment in the pure breezes of the forest, and no less a power in the tender word of faith and love spoken by the young priest in his fervent desire to lead this poor straying one into the way of light and love.

It is said that raindrops can wear a hollow in the hardest stone, and the waves of the sea can smooth and round the jagged rocks; so did the dew of mercy falling upon little Helga, soften all that was hard and smooth all that was rough in her. Not that these effects were yet to be seen; she did not even know that they had taken place, any more than the buried seed lying in the earth knows that the refreshing showers and the warm sunbeams will cause it to flourish and bloom.

As the mother's song unconsciously falls upon the child's heart, it stammers the words after her without understanding them; but later they crystallize into thoughts, and in time become clear. In this way the "Word: also worked here in the heart of Helga.

They rode out of the wood, over a heath, and again through trackless forests. Toward evening they met a band of robbers.

"Where hast thou stolen this beautiful child?" they cried, stopping the horse and pulling down the two riders, for they were a numerous party.

The priest had no weapon but the knife which he had taken from little Helga, and with this he struck out right and left. One of the robbers raised his ax to strike him, but the Christian succeeded in springing on one side, or he would certainly have been hit; but the blade flew into the horse's neck, so that the blood gushed forth, and it fell to the ground dead. Then little Helga, as if roused from a long, deep trance, rushed forward and threw herself on to the gasping horse. The priest placed himself in front of her as a shield and defense; but one of the robbers swung his iron club with such force at his head that the blood and the brains were scattered about, and he fell dead upon the ground.

The robbers seized little Helga by her white arms, but the sun was just going down, and as the last rays vanished she was changed into the form of a frog. A greenish-white mouth stretched half over her face; her arms became thin and slimy; while broad hands, with webbed fingers, spread themselves out like fans. The robbers in terror let her go, and she stood among them a hideous monster; and, according to frog nature, she bounded away with great leaps as high as herself, and disappeared in the thicket. Then the robbers perceived that this must be Loki's evil spirit or some other witchcraft, and they hurried away affrighted.

The full moon had risen and was shining in all its splendor when poor little Helga, in the form of a frog, crept out of the thicket. She stopped by the body of the Christian priest and the dead horse; she looked at them with eyes which seemed to weep;

a sob came from the toad like that of a child bursting into tears. She threw herself down, first upon one, and then on the other; and brought water in her hand, which, from being large and webbed, formed a cup. This she sprinkled them with; but they were dead, and dead they must remain! This she understood. Soon wild animals would come and devour them; but no, that should never be; so she dug into the ground as deep as she could; she wished to dig a grave for them. She had nothing but the branch of a tree and her two hands, and she tore the web between her fingers till the blood ran from them. She soon saw that the task would be beyond her, so she fetched fresh water and washed the face of the dead man, and strewed fresh green leaves over it. She also brought large boughs to cover him, and scattered dried leaves between the branches. Then she brought the heaviest stones she could carry, and laid them over the dead body, filling up the spaces with moss. Now she thought the mound was strong and secure enough, but the difficult task had employed the whole night; the sun was just rising, and there stood little Helga in all her beauty with bleeding hands and maidenly tears for the first time on her blushing cheeks.

It was in this transformation as if two natures were struggling in her; she trembled and glanced round as if she were just awaking from a troubled dream. She leaned for support against a slender beech, and at last climbed to the topmost branches like a cat and seated herself firmly upon them. She sat there for the whole livelong day like a frightened squirrel in the solitude of the wood where all is still, and dead, as they say!

Dead—well there flew a couple of butterflies whirling round and round each other, and close by were some anthills each with its hundreds of busy little creatures swarming to and fro. In the air danced countless midges, and swarm upon swarm of flies, ladybirds, dragonflies with golden wings, and other little winged creatures. The earthworm crept forth from the moist ground, and the moles—but excepting these all was still and dead around; when people say this they don't quite understand what they mean. None noticed little Helga but a flock of jackdaws which flew chattering round the tree where she sat. They hopped along the branch toward her boldly inquisitive, but a glance from her eye was enough to drive them away. They could not make her out though, any more than she could understand herself.

When the evening drew near and the sun began to sink, the approaching transformation roused her to fresh exertion. She slipped down gently from the tree, and when the last sunbeam was extinguished she sat there once more, the shriveled up frog with her torn, webbed hands; but her eyes now shone with a new beauty which they had hardly possessed in all the pride of her loveliness. These were the gentlest and tenderest maiden's eyes which now shone out of the face of the frog. They bore witness to the existence of deep feeling and a human heart; and the beauteous eyes overflowed with tears, weeping precious drops that lightened the heart.

The cross made of branches, the last work of him who now was dead and cold, still lay by the grave. Little Helga took it up, the thought came unconsciously, and she placed it between the stones which covered man and horse. At the sad recollection her tears burst forth again, and in this mood she traced the same sign in the earth round the grave—and as she formed with both hands the sign of the cross, the webbed skin fell away from her fingers like a torn glove. She washed her hands at the spring and gazed in astonishment at their delicate whiteness. Again she made the holy sign in the air, between herself and the dead man; her lips trembled, her tongue moved, and the name which she in her ride through the forest had so often heard, rose to her lips, and she uttered the words "Jesus Christ."

The frog's skin fell away from her, she was the beautiful young maiden, but her head bent wearily and her limbs required rest. She slept. But her sleep was short, she was awakened at midnight, before her stood the dead horse prancing and full of life, which shone forth from his eyes and his wounded neck. Close by his side appeared the murdered Christian priest, "more beautiful than Baldur," the Viking's wife might indeed have said, and yet he was surrounded by flames of fire.

There was such earnestness in his large, mild eyes, and such righteous judgment in his penetrating glance which pierced into the remotest corners of her heart. Little Helga trembled, and every memory within her was awakened as if it had been the day of Judgment. Every kindness which had ever been shown her, every loving word which had been said to her, came vividly before her. She now understood that it was love which had sustained her in those days of trial, through which all creatures formed of dust and clay, soul and spirit, must wrestle and struggle. She acknowledged that she had but followed whither she was called, had done nothing for herself; all had been given her. She bent now in lowly humility, and full of shame, before Him who could read every impulse of her heart; and in that moment she felt the purifying flame of the Holy Spirit thrill through her soul.

"Thou daughter of earth!" said the Christian martyr, "out of the earth art thou come, from the earth shalt thou rise again! The sunlight within thee shall consciously return to its origin; not the beams of the actual sun, but those from God! No soul will be lost, things temporal are full of weariness, but eternity is life giving. I come from the land of the dead; thou also must one day journey through the deep valleys to reach the radiant mountain summits where dwell grace and all perfection. I cannot lead thee to Hedeby for Christian baptism; first must thou break the watery shield that covers the deep morass, and bring forth from its depths the living author of thy being and thy life; thou must first carry out thy vocation before thy consecration may take place!"

Then he lifted her up on to the horse, and gave her a golden censer like those she had seen in the Viking's hall. A fragrant perfume arose from it, and the open wound on the martyr's forehead gleamed like a radiant diadem. He took the cross from the grave, holding it high above him, while they rode rapidly through the air; across the murmuring woods, and over the heights where the mighty warriors of old lay buried, each seated on his dead war horse. These strong men of war arose and rode out to the summits of the mounds; the broad golden circlets round their foreheads gleaming in the moonlight, and their cloaks fluttering in the wind. The great dragon hoarding his treasure raised his head to look at them, and whole hosts of dwarfs peeped forth from their hillocks, swarming with red, green, and blue lights, like sparks from the ashes of burnt paper.

Away they flew over wood and heath, rivers and pools, up north toward the Wild Bog; arrived here they hovered round in great circles. The martyr raised high the cross, it shone like gold, and his lips chanted the holy mass. Little Helga sang with him as a child joins in its mother's song. She swung the censer, and from it issued a fragrance of the altar so strong and so wonder-working that the reeds and rushes burst into blossom, and numberless flower stems shot up from the bottomless depths; everything that had life within it lifted itself up and blossomed. The water lilies spread themselves over the surface of the pool like a carpet of wrought flowers, and on this carpet lay a sleeping woman. She was young and beautiful; little Helga fancied she saw herself, her picture mirrored in the quiet pool. It was her mother she saw the wife of the Marsh King, the princess from the river Nile.

The martyred priest commanded the sleeping woman to be lifted up on to the horse, but the animal sank beneath the burden, as though it had no more substance than a winding sheet floating on the wind; but the sign of the cross gave strength to the phantom, and all three rode on through the air to dry ground. Just then the cock crew from the Viking's hall, and the vision melted away in the mist which was driven along by the wind, but mother and daughter stood side by side.

"Is it myself I see reflected in the deep water?" said the mother.

"Do I see myself mirrored in a bright shield?" said the daughter. But as they approached and clasped each other heart to heart, the mother's heart beat the fastest, and she understood.

"My child! my own heart's blossom! my lotus out of the deep waters!" and she wept over her daughter; her tears were a new baptism of love and life for little Helga. "I came hither in a swan's plumage, and here I threw if off," said the mother. "I sank down into the bog, which closed around me. Some power always dragged me down, deeper and deeper. I felt the hand of sleep pressing upon my eyelids. I fell asleep, and I dreamt—I seemed to be again in the vast Egyptian Pyramid; but still before me stood the moving alder stump which had frightened me on the surface of the bog. I gazed at the fissures of the bark and they shone out in bright colors and turned to hieroglyphs; it was the mummy's wrappings I was looking at. The coverings burst asunder, and out of them walked the mummy king of a thousand years ago, black as pitch, black as the shining wood snail or the slimy mud of the swamp. Whether it were the Mummy King or the Marsh King I knew not. He threw his arms around me, and I felt that I must die. When life came back to me I felt something warm upon my bosom; a little bird fluttering its wings and twittering. It flew from my bosom high up toward the heavy dark canopy, but a long green ribbon still bound it to me; I heard and understood its notes of longing: 'Freedom! Sunshine! To the Father!' I remembered my own father in the sunlit land of my home, my life, and my love! And I loosened the ribbon and let it flutter away—home to my father. Since that hour I have dreamt no more; I must have slept a long and heavy sleep till this hour, when sweet music and fragrant odors awoke me and set me free."

Where did now the green ribbon flutter which bound the mother's heart to the wings of the bird? Only the stork had seen it. The ribbon was the green stem, the bow the gleaming flower which cradled the little baby, now grown up to her full beauty, and once more resting on her mother's breast. While they stood there pressed heart to heart the stork was wheeling above their heads in great circles; at length he flew away to his nest and brought back the swan plumages so long cherished there. He threw one over each of them; the feathers closed over them closely, and mother and daughter rose into the air as two white swans.

"Now let us talk!" said the father stork; "for we can understand each other's language, even if one sort of bird has a different shaped beak from another. It is the most fortunate thing in the world that you appeared this evening. Tomorrow we should have been off, Mother and I and the young ones. We are going to fly southwards. Yes, you may look at me! I am an old friend from the Nile, so is Mother too; her heart is not so sharp as her beak! She always said that the princess would take care of herself! I and the young ones carried the swans' plumage up here! How delighted I am, and how lucky it is that I am still here; as soon as the day dawns we will set off, a great company of storks. We will fly in front, you had better follow us and then you won't lose your way, and we will keep an eye upon you."

"And the lotus flower which I was to take with me," said the Egyptian Princess, "flies by my side in a swan's plumage. I take the flower of my heart with me, and so the riddle is solved. Now for home! home!"

But Helga said she could not leave the Danish land without seeing her loving foster mother once more, the Viking's wife. For in Helga's memory now rose up every happy recollection, every tender word and every tear her foster mother had shed over her, and it almost seemed as if she loved this mother best.

"Yes, we must go to the Viking's hall," said the father stork; "Mother and the young ones are waiting for us there. How they will open their eyes and flap their wings! Mother doesn't say much; she is somewhat short and abrupt, but she means very well. Now I will make a great clattering to let them know we are coming!"

So he clattered with his beak, and he and the swans flew off to the Viking's hall.

They all lay in a deep sleep within; the Viking's wife had gone late to rest, for she was in great anxiety about little Helga, who had not been seen for three days. She had disappeared with the Christian priest, and she must have helped him away; it was her horse which was missing from the stable. By what power had this been brought to pass? The Viking's wife thought over all the many miracles which were said to have been performed by the "White Christ," and by those who believed in Him and followed Him. All these thoughts took form in her dreams, and it seemed to her that she was still awake, sitting thoughtfully upon her bed while darkness reigned without. A storm arose; she heard the rolling of the waves east and west of her from the North Sea, and from the waters of the Cattegat. The monstrous serpent which, according to her faith, encompassed the earth in the depths of the ocean, was trembling in convulsions from dread of "Ragnarok," the night of the gods. He personified the day of Judgment when everything should pass away, even the great gods themselves. The Gialler horn sounded, and away over the rainbow rode the gods, clad in steel to fight their last battle; before them flew the shield maidens, the Valkyries, and the ranks were closed by the phantoms of the dead warriors. The whole atmosphere shone in the radiance of the northern lights, but darkness conquered in the end. It was a terrible hour, and in her dream little Helga sat close beside the frightened woman, crouching on the floor in the form of the hideous frog. She trembled and crept closer to her foster mother who took her on her knee, and in her love pressed her to her bosom notwithstanding the hideous frog's skin. And the air resounded with the slashing of sword and club, and the whistling of arrows as though a fierce hailstorm were passing over them. The hour had come when heaven and earth were to pass away, the stars to fall, and everything to succumb to Surtur's fire—and yet a new earth and a new heaven would arise, and fields of corn would wave where the seas now rolled over the golden sands. The God whom none might name would reign, and to Him would ascent Baldur the mild, the loving, redeemed from the kingdom of the dead—he was coming—the Viking's wife saw him plainly, she knew his face—it was that of the Christian priest, their prisoner. "White Christ," she cried aloud, and as she named the name she pressed a kiss upon the forehead of the loathsome toad; the frog's skin fell away and before her stood little Helga in all the radiance of her beauty, gentle as she had never been before and with beaming eyes. She kissed her foster mother's hands, and blessed her for all the care and love she had shown in the days of her trial and misery. She thanked her for the thoughts she had instilled into her, and for naming the name which she now repeated, "White Christ!" Little Helga rose up as a great white swan and spread her wings, with the rushing sound of a flock of birds of passage on the wing.

The Viking's wife was awakened by the rushing of wings outside; she knew it was the time when the storks took their flight, and it was these she heard. She wanted to see them once more and to bid them farewell, so she got up and went out on to the balcony; she saw stork upon stork sitting on the roofs of the outbuildings round the courtyard, and flocks of them were flying round and round in great circles. Just in front of her, on the edge of the well where little Helga so often had frightened her with her wildness, sat two white swans, who gazed at her with their wise eyes. Then she remembered her dream, which still seemed quite real to her. She thought of little Helga in the form of a swan. She thought of the Christian priest and suddenly a great joy arose in her heart. The swans flapped their wings and bent their heads as if to greet her, and the Viking's wife stretched out her arms toward them as if she understood all about it, and she smiled at them with tears in her eyes.

"We are not going to wait for the swans," said the mother stork. "If they want to travel with us they must come. We can't dawdle here till the plovers start! It is very nice to travel as we do, the whole family together, not like the chaffinches and the ruffs, when the males and females fly separately; it's hardly decent! And why are those swans flapping their wings like that?"

"Well, everyone flies in his own way," said the father stork. "The swans fly in an oblique line, the cranes in the form of a triangle, and the plovers in a curved line like a snake."

"Don't talk about snakes while we are flying up here," said the mother stork. "It puts desires into the young one's heads which they can't gratify."

"Are those the high mountains I used to hear about?" asked Helga in the swan's plumage.

"Those are thunder clouds driving along beneath us," said her mother.

"What are those white clouds that rise so high?" again enquired Helga.

"Those are mountains covered with perpetual snows that you see yonder," said her mother, as they flew across the Alps down toward the blue Mediterranean.

"Africa's land! Egypt's strand!" sang the daughter of the Nile in her joy, as from far above in her swan's plumage, her eye fell upon the narrow waving yellow line, her birthplace. The other birds saw it too and hastened their flight.

"I smell the Nile mud and the frogs," said the mother stork. "I am tingling all over. Now, you will have something nice to taste, and something to see too. There are the marabous, the ibis, and the crane. They all belong to our family, but they are not nearly so handsome as we are; they are very stuck up though, especially the ibis, they have been so spoilt by the Egyptians. They make mummies of him, and stuff him with spices. I would rather be stuffed with living frogs, and so would you, and so you shall be! Better have something in your crops while you are alive, than have a great fuss made over you after you are dead. That is my opinion, and I am always right."

"The storks have come back," was said in the great house on the Nile, where its lord lay in the great hall on his downy cushions covered with a leopard skin, scarcely alive, and yet not dead either, waiting and hoping for the lotus flower from the deep morass in the north.

Relatives and servants stood round his couch, when two great white swans who had come with the storks flew into the hall. They threw off their dazzling plumage, and there stood two beautiful women as like each other as twin drops of dew. They bent over the pale withered old man, throwing back their long hair.

As little Helga bent over her grandfather, the color came back to his cheeks and new life returned to his limbs. The old man rose with health and energy renewed; his daughter and granddaughter clasped him in their arms, as if with a joyous morning greeting after a long troubled night.

Joy reigned throughout the house and in the stork's nest too, but there the rejoicing was chiefly over the abundance of food, especially the swarms of frogs. And while the sages hastily sketched the story of the two princesses and the flower of healing, which brought such joy and blessing to the land, the parent storks told the same story in their own way to their family; but only when they had all satisfied their appetites, or they would have had something better to do than to listen to stories.

"Surely you will be made something at last," whispered the mother stork. "It wouldn't be reasonable otherwise."

"Oh, what should I be made?" said the father stork; "and what have I done? Nothing at all!"

"You have done more than all the others! Without you and the young ones the two princesses would never have seen Egypt again, nor would the old man have recovered his health. You will become something. They will at least give you a doctor's degree, and our young ones will be born with the title, and their young ones after them. Why, you look like an Egyptian doctor already, at least in my eyes!"

And now the learned men and the sages set to work to propound the inner principle, as they called it, that lay at the root of the matter. "Love is the food of life," was their text. Then came the explanations. "The princess was the warm sunbeam; she went down to the Marsh King, and from their meeting sprang forth the blossom."

"I can't exactly repeat the words," said the father stork. He had been listening on the roof, and now wanted to tell them all about it in the nest. "What they said was so involved and so clever that they not only received rank, but presents too; even the head cook had a mark of distinction—most likely for the soup!"

"And what did you get?" asked the mother stork. "They ought not to forget the most important person, and that is what you are; the sages have only cackled about it all. But your turn will come, no doubt!"

Late at night, when the whole happy household were wrapped in peaceful slumbers, there was still one watcher. It was not Father stork, although he stood up in the nest on one leg like a sentry asleep at his post. No, it was little Helga. She was watching, bending out over the balcony in the clear air, gazing at the shining stars, bigger and purer in their radiance than she had ever seen them in the north; and yet they were the same. She thought of the Viking's wife by the Wild Bog; she thought of her foster mother's gentle eyes, and the tears she had shed over the poor frog child, who now stood in the bright starlight and delicious spring air by the waters of the Nile. She thought of the love in the heathen woman's breast, the love she had lavished on a miserable creature, who in human guise was a wild animal, and when in the form of an animal was hateful to the sight and to the touch. She looked at the shining stars, and remembered the dazzling light on the forehead of the martyred priest as he flew over moorland and forest. The tones of his voice came back to her, and words that he had said while she sat overwhelmed and crushed—words concerning the sublime source of love, the highest love embracing all generations of mankind. What had not been won and achieved by this love? Day and night little Helga was absorbed in the thought of her happiness; she entirely lost herself in the contemplation of it, like a child who turns hurriedly from the giver to examine the beautiful gifts. Happy she was indeed, and her happiness seemed ever growing; more might come, would come. In these thoughts she indulged, until she thought no more of the Giver. It was in the wantonness of youth that she thus sinned. Her eyes sparkled with pride, but suddenly she was roused from her vain dream. She heard a great clatter in the courtyard below, and looking out, saw two great ostriches rushing hurriedly round in circles; never before had she seen this great, heavy, clumsy bird, which looked as if its wings had been clipped, and the birds themselves had the appearance of having been roughly used. She asked what had happened to them, and for the first time heard the legend the Egyptians tell concerning the ostrich.

Once, they say, the ostriches were a beautiful and glorious race of birds with large, strong wings. One evening the great birds of the forest said to it, "Brother, shall we tomorrow, God willing, go down to the river to drink?" And the ostrich answered, "I will!"

At the break of day, then, they flew off, first rising high in the air toward the sun, the eye of God; still higher and higher the ostrich flew, far in front of the other birds, in its pride flying close up to the light. He trusted in his own strength, and not on that of the Giver; he would not say "God willing!" But the avenging angel drew back the veil from the flaming ocean of sunlight, and in a moment the wings of the proud bird were burnt, and he sank miserably to the earth. Since that time the ostrich and his race have never been able to rise in the air; he can only fly terror stricken along the ground, or round and round in narrow circles. It is a warning to mankind, reminding us in every thought and action to say "God willing!"

Helga thoughtfully and seriously bent her head and looked at the hunted ostrich, noticed its fear and its miserable pride at the sight of its own great shadow on the white moonlit wall. Her thoughts grew graver and more earnest. A life so rich in joy had already been given her; what more was to come? The best of all perhaps—"God willing!"

Early in the spring, when the storks were again about to take flight to the north, little Helga took off her gold bracelet, and, scratching her name on it, beckoned to Father stork and put it round his neck. She told him to take it to the Viking's wife, who would see by it that her foster daughter still lived, was happy, and had not forgotten her.

"It is a heavy thing to carry!" thought Father stork, as it slipped on to his neck; "but neither gold nor honor are to be thrown upon the highway! The stork brings good luck, they say up there!"

"You lay gold, and I lay eggs," said Mother stork; "but you only lay once and I lay every year. But no one appreciates us; I call it very mortifying!"

"One always has the consciousness of one's own worth, though, Mother!" said Father stork.

"But you can't hang it outside," said Mother stork; "it neither gives a fair wind nor a full meal!" And they took their departure.

The little nightingale singing in the tamarind bushes was also going north soon; Helga had often heard it singing by the Wild Bog, so she determined to send a message by it too. She knew the bird language from having worn a swan's plumage, and she had kept it up by speaking to the storks and the swallows. The nightingale understood her quite well, so she begged it to fly to the beech wood in Jutland, where she had made the grave of stones and branches; she bade it tell all the other little birds to guard the grave and to sing over it. The nightingale flew away—and time flew away too.

In the autumn an eagle, perched on one of the Pyramids, saw a gorgeous train of heavily-laden camels and men clad in armor riding fiery Arabs steeds as white as silver with quivering red nostrils and flowing manes reaching to the ground. A royal prince from Arabia, as handsome as a prince should be, was arriving at the stately mansion where now the storks' nest stood empty; its inhabitants were still in their northern home; but they would soon now return—nay, on the very day when the rejoicings were at their height they returned. There were bridal festivities and little Helga was the bride clad in rich silk and many jewels. The bridegroom was the young prince from Arabia, and they sat together at the upper end of the table between her mother and her grandfather.

But Helga was not looking at the bridegroom's handsome face round which his black beard curled, nor did she look into his fiery dark eyes which were fixed upon hers. She was gazing up at a brilliant twinkling star which was beaming in the heavens.

Just then there was a rustle of great wings in the air outside; the storks had come back. And the old couple, tired as they were and needing rest, flew straight down to the railing of the veranda; they knew nothing about the festivities. They had heard on the frontiers of the country that little Helga had had them painted on the wall, for they belonged to the story of her life.

"It was prettily done of her," said Father stork.

"It is little enough," said Mother stork; "they could hardly do less."

When Helga saw them she rose from the table and went out on to the veranda to stroke their wings. The old storks bowed their heads and the very youngest ones looked on and felt honored. And Helga looked up at the shining star which seemed to grow brighter and purer; between herself and the star floated a form purer even than the air and therefore visible to her. It floated quite close to her and she saw that it was the martyred priest, he also had come to her great festival—come even from the heavenly kingdom.

"The glory and bliss yonder, far outshines these earthly splendors," he said.

Little Helga prayed more earnestly and meekly than she had ever done before, that for one single moment she might gaze into the Kingdom of Heaven. Then she felt herself lifted up above the earth in a stream of sweet sounds and thoughts. The unearthly music was not only around her, it was within her. No words can express it.

"Now we must return; you will be missed," said the martyr.

"Only one glance more," she pleaded; "only one short moment more."

"We must return to earth; the guests are departing."

"Only one look—the last."

Little Helga stood once again on the veranda, but all the torches outside were extinguished and the lights in the banqueting hall were out too; the storks were gone; no guests were to be seen; no bridegroom—all had vanished in those short three minutes.

A great dread seized upon Helga; she walked through the great empty hall into the next chamber where strange warriors were sleeping. She opened a side door which led into her own room, but she found herself in a garden, which had never been there before. Red gleams were in the sky, dawn was approaching. Only three minutes in Heaven, and a whole night on earth had passed away.

Then she saw the storks; she called to them in her own language. Father stork turned his head, listened, and came up to her.

"You speak our language," he said. "What do you want? Why do you come here, you strange woman?"

"It is I, it is Helga; don't you know me? We were talking to each other on the veranda three minutes ago."

"That is a mistake," said the stork; "you must have dreamt it."

"No, no," she said, and she reminded him of the Viking's stronghold, and the Wild Bog, and their journey together.

Father stork blinked his eyes and said, "Why, that is a very old story; I believe it happened in the time of my great-great-grandmother. Yes, there certainly was a princess in Egypt who came from the Danish land, but she disappeared on her wedding night many hundred years ago. You may read all about it here, on the monument in the garden. There are both storks and swans carved on it, and you are at the top yourself, all in white marble."

And so it was: Helga understood all about it now and sank upon her knees.

The sun burst forth, and as in former times the frog's skin fell away before his beams and revealed the beautiful girl, so now, in the baptism of light, a vision of beauty, brighter and purer than the air—a ray of light—rose to the Father. The earthly body dropped away in dust—only a withered lotus flower lay where she had stood.

"Well, that is a new ending to the story," said Father stork; "I hadn't expected that, but I like it very well."

"What will the young ones say about it?" asked Mother stork.

"Ah, that is a very important matter," said Father stork.

—Hans Christian Andersen

Part Two

Water Song, First Part
(A Pact with the Gulls)

LOVE I TAI LAKE MOST
With its inlets green;
My shoes and staff while they last,
Ten times a day I'll go.
My Heron and Gull friends!
From to-day's pact onwards
Mix freely shall we.
O where is the Stork?
Bring him along please.

Clear the weeds,
Sweep the growth,
Green moss stay:

The prying fish our folly may well mock
And wonder why my cup I raise.
As of yore the waste and marsh abide,
Yet same the moon and breeze this night,
What joy and rue our lives disclose!
Too few green shades on east bank?
Yes, we must plant more willows.

—Hsin Ch'I-Chi
from *Poems from China*

Jeremiah 8:7

EVEN THE STORK IN the heavens knows her times;
And the turtledove, swallow, and crane keep the time of their
coming; but my people know not the ordinance of the Lord.

Holy Bible—Revised Standard Version

Migration

THEY SAY THE CRANES LEAVE
with the first tail wind.
A south wind which blows
across the stubble
like the warm breath
of their wings
cupped in my stiff, old fingers.

I think I'll go with them
this year
just to feel the sun
on my back and
the beaten wind
against my face.

—Anne Meredith McCollister

The Fowls of Heaven
or
A History of Birdes

...THE OTHER THING observed in (the crane's) flight is the form and fashion wherein they rank themselves, for while the air is calm and not troubled by boisterous winds, they fly triangularly like the Greek letter *Iambda*, pointed before and forked behind, that so before them the air may be cut and pierced more easily, but behind them, the open passage foremost and hindmost may be benefited by the blast thereof.

...They change places in their course...every one in his order, after a certain distance of time and place.

—Edward Topsell
from *The Fowls of Heaven or A History of Birdes*

The Wolf and the Crane

A WOLF DEVOURED HIS prey so ravenously that a bone got stuck in his throat, and in extreme agony, he ran and howled throughout the forest, beseeching every animal he met to pull out the bone. He even offered a generous reward to anyone who succeeded in pulling it out. Moved by his pleas as well as the prospect of the money, a crane ventured her long neck down the wolf's throat and drew out the bone. She then modestly asked for the promised reward, but the wolf just grinned and bared his teeth.

"Ungrateful creature!" he replied with seeming indignation. "How dare you ask for any other reward than your life? After all, you're among the very few who can say that you've put your head into the jaws of a wolf and were permitted to draw it out in safety."

Moral: Expect no reward when you serve the wicked, and be thankful if you escape injury for your pains.

—Aesop's Fables

Hymn

THEY GATHERED BLACK
under the purple heavens east,
at first, in twos and fours,
and then in full measure,
notes sifted from the sheltered hand
of God,
laying down upon the golden sky
the full throat of ten thousand cranes
calling for family.

—Anne Meredith McCollister

St. Columba and the Crane

A ND ANOTHER TIME IT BEFELL, while the Saint was living on Iona, that he called one of the brethren to him, to speak to him. "Go thou," he said, "three days from now to the west of this island at dawn, and sit above the shore and wait: for when the third hour before sunset is past, there shall come flying from the northern coasts of Ireland a stranger guest, a crane, wind tossed and driven far from her course in the high air: tired out and weary she will fall on the beach at thy feet and lie there, her strength nigh gone: tenderly lift her and carry her to the steading near by: make her welcome there and cherish her with all care for three days and nights; and when the three days are ended, refreshed and loath to tarry longer with us in our exile, she shall take flight again towards that old sweet land of Ireland whence she came, in pride of strength once more: and if I commend her so earnestly to thy charge, it is that in that countryside where thou and I were reared, she too was nested."

The brother obeyed: and on the third day, with the third hour before sunset was past, stood as he was bidden, in wait for the coming of the promised guest: and when she had come and lay fallen on the beach, he lifted her and carried her ailing to the steading, and fed her, famished as she was. And on his return that evening to the monastery the Saint spoke to him, not as one questioning but as one speaks of a thing past. "May God bless thee, my son," said he, "for thy kind tending of this pilgrim guest: that shall make no long stay in her exile, but when three suns have set shall turn back to her own land."

And the thing fell out even as the Saint had foretold. For when her three days housing was ended, and as her host stood by, she rose in first flight from the earth into high heaven, and after a while at gaze to spy out her aerial way, took her straight flight above the quiet sea, and so to Ireland through the tranquil weather.

—St. Columba
from *Beasts and Saints*

The Crane's Feather

P EOPLE TELL, PEOPLE SING about the brave hunter Yudjian; they tell, they sing about his little brother Hodjugur, about their lives and the events that befell them.

The two brothers lived without a mother and without a father. The older brother was both father and mother to the younger. And this is how they lived: when the sun had barely lifted its edge over the earth, the older brother, Yudjian, would already be out hunting in the woods. When the sun rose higher, the younger brother, Hodjugur, would get up, sweep the yard, feed the horses and the cows. In the evening, he would start a fire in the fireplace, and by then Yudjian would be back from the hunt.

Yudjian was a brave and skillful hunter. Before dawn, he drove fur animals from their lairs. At dawn, he chased the elk. At sunset, he wrestled with the bear. And his arrows never missed a wolf. In the brothers' yurt there were many soft skins, and fat and meat were always plentiful.

One day, as always, Yudjian went out to hunt. Young Hodjugur, as always, remained at home. He went out of the yurt to sweep the yard and heard a honking in the sky. He looked up. Seven white cranes were circling over him. On the side of the sun, their wings glowed warmly pink. In the shadow they turned a delicate pale blue. Hodjugur waved his hand to the cranes, and they came lower.

"Is anyone else at home-home?" they asked.

"I am home alone-alone," he answered. "My older brother is out hunting."

The cranes asked one another:

"Shall we play for a while with the boy, sisters? He won't be lonely, and we shall have some fun, too."

They came down into the yard, walked all around it on their long legs, then threw off their white-feathered skins and turned into beautiful maidens. They started merry games with Hodjugur. They raced, played hide and seek, danced, and sang. They ran into the yurt and looked at everything. All day they played and laughed. When the sun began to set they hurriedly put on their white-feathered skins, turned back into cranes, flapped their wings, and took off.

Soon Yudjian returned with the day's catch.

He looked around-the yard had not been swept, the hungry cows lowed in the barn, the thirsty horses neighed in the stable. The wood had not been chopped, water had not been brought, the fire had not been started.

"Why haven't you done your day's work? he asked Hodjugur.

"I'm sorry-sorry, older brother! said Hodjugur. "I slept all day, I thought the sunset was the dawn."

The older brother laughed and was not angry. Together they quickly finished the chores. They fed the cows, watered the horses, and cooked their own food. After eating, they went to bed.

The next morning, as soon as his brother was out of the yard, Hodjugur jumped up. He did not idle the hours away on the soft skins. He ran out of the yurt and looked up at the sky. And the cranes were already there, circling over him, beneath the sky, above the yard.

"He is gone! My brother is gone!" Hodjugur cried to them. "Come down, hurry!"

The cranes came down and turned into maidens. And they played the same games as the day before. Again Hodjugur did not notice how the day went by. In parting, the cranes said to him:

"Don't tell your brother about us. If you say a single word, we shall not come back!"

They flew away. Like large snowflakes they melted in the sky. And Hodjugur hurried to catch up with his chores. But his brother was already on the way home, leading an elk by his nostrils.

Yudjian looked around and saw again that nothing had been done. This time he was angry.

"Will you tell me that you overslept again?"

"I will," said Hodjugur.

Yudjian gave Hodjugur a thrashing, not in anger, but to teach him a lesson. But to himself he thought: something is behind it, there must be a reason for this. The boy was never lazy before, he did everything that needed to be done with good will.

In the morning, Yudjian rose as usual. He took his bow and arrows, left the yurt, but did not go into the woods. He threw himself upon the ground and turned into a flea. Then he hid in a crack in the fence and waited.

Ah-h, Hodjugur was not asleep at all, he was not idling in his furry bed. He ran out of the yurt, stopped in the middle of the yard next to the hitching post, and raised his head. The flea thrust out its head and looked up too. A flock of cranes was circling in the sky, saying human words in their own cry:

"Hey, little Hodjugur, is your brother gone?"

"He's gone, he's gone!" cried Hodjugur, gaily waving his arms. "Come down, come down, hurry!"

But the cranes would not come down.

"Why is your yard darkened by shadow? Why is your yurt, why is your fire hidden by a dark fog?"

"It only seems so to you," answered Hodjugur. "The sun has not yet risen very high. You can see it from up above, but it has not come here as yet."

"So your brother is not home?" the cranes asked once again.

"No, no! He has already reached the woods and found his quarry, he is already tracking it!"

Seven white cranes came down into the yard. They turned into maidens and hung their feathered skins on the hitching post.

Yudjian stared at them as though bewitched. Each one was beautiful, but the seventh was the loveliest of them all. The crane girls raced one another, but she was the fastest of all. They danced, but she had the lightest step of all, as if her feet never touched the ground. And Hodjugur stayed closest to her, as if she were his favorite companion.

The day began to turn into evening, and the maidens said to Hodjugur:

"Your brother will come home soon, it is time for us to go."

And Yudjian sat in his crack, thinking:

My brother spoke the truth. I have not noticed either how the day ran into evening. It is like a marvelous dream!

The maidens hurried to the hitching post and stretched their hands to get their skins. But the flea had hopped out of its hiding place and got there first. And Yudjian turned back into himself and seized the skin of the seventh maiden.

Six white cranes rose up into the sky. One girl sobbed on the ground, begging the hunter to return her skin. But Yudjian said:

"I looked at you all day, rejoicing in your beauty. Now take a look at me. If I don't please you, take the skin and fly wherever you will. But if I do, stay here and be my wife."

The maiden looked at him through her tears. Her tears dried and she smiled at him.

"I will stay," she said quietly.

Yudjian asked:

"What shall I do with the skin? Shall I hang it on a pole in the yurt, or burn it in the fireplace?"

The maiden turned white like newly fallen snow.

"Don't throw it into the fire! If you do, misfortune will befall me. And do not hang it in the yurt. On a spring day I may be overcome with sudden longing for the sky and forget everything on earth. I will not pity you, I will not pity myself, I will fly away and away! Hide it so that no one's hands will touch it, no one's eyes will see it."

Yudjian hid the white-feathered skin in a chest bound with iron. He locked the chest with three locks, and hung the keys high on a peg by the door.

And Yudjian and the maiden lived happily as man and wife. As soon as they awakened, they spoke kind words of greeting to each other. In the morning the wife prepared her husband's hunting gear and wept as though he were leaving her forever. In the evening Yudjian hurried home as though he had not seen his wife for a whole year.

The yurt was always clean and tidy. A welcoming fire burned always in the hearth, the animals were fed and watered, the yard was swept.

One thing was bad: Hodjugur had gotten altogether spoiled and out of hand. In the past, he had all the household chores to do, but now the young wife did everything. And all day long the boy ran about wild, forever thinking up new mischief. The autumn passed, the winter went by.

One day the young woman went out for water. She came down to the river and forgot what she had come for. The clear sky turned the water blue, the songbirds were building their nests. Everything was in bloom. For a long time she stood motionless. Then she shook herself, filled her vessel with water, and turned homeward.

But while she was away, the boy Hodjugur was in the yurt, looking high and low for his brother's old bow and arrow. He had long wanted to become a hunter, to help his brother, but Yudjian kept telling him that he was still too young and did not know how to use a bow and arrow. And Hodjugur decided that it was time for him to learn. If he could find the bow and arrows, he would practice in secret and surprise his brother.

Hodjugur turned everything in the yurt upside down, but could not find what he was looking for.

Could they be in the chest? he wondered.

He took the three keys from the peg, unlocked the three locks, and raised the heavy lid. He did not find the bow and arrows, but he found the white-feathered crane skin. He took it out and admired it: such pretty feathers!

At this moment his sister-in-law came in. She stopped still and looked.

"Give me the skin," she said.

Her voice did not seem to be her own, it sounded like the honking of cranes, far, far away.

Hodjugur hid the skin behind his back.

"I will not give it to you," he said. "Yudjian had good reason to lock it in the chest. I found it by chance, and I will put it back at once."

"Just let me hold it for a moment," the woman begged. "I will give you my golden earrings."

"I am not a girl! What do I need your golden earrings for?"

"I will give you a belt embroidered with silver."

"A man does not need a woman's belt."

"I will give you a knife with a carved handle, with an inlaid sheath."

Hodjugur's eyes glittered.

"A knife is a fine thing for a hunter!" said the boy. "Let me have it!"

He seized the knife and gave her the skin.

She threw it over her shoulders and turned into a white crane. She went out into the yard, stepping carefully on her long legs, afraid to spread her wings, afraid they would lift her from the ground and carry her off into the sky. Yudjian would miss her, and she herself would sicken with longing for him.

She was just going to take off the skin when she heard cranes calling. Six cranes were circling above the yard, calling her to join them. She leaped up with a sorrowful cry and spread her wide wings.

Hodjugur ran out when he heard her. Frightened, he ran after her and tried to catch her by the wing, but he was too late. The crane rose up, and only a single feather remained in his hand.

Seven cranes circled over the yurt for the last time. Then they rose and rose, higher and higher, until they disappeared behind a cloud.

Hodjugur followed them with his eyes, then he shook his head and said:

"And she only asked to hold it in her hands for a moment! Never again will I believe a woman!"

He sat down in the middle of the yard, put down the feather next to him, and began to play with the knife. And this was how his brother, who returned from hunting earlier than usual, found him.

"Where did you get the knife?" he asked.

"Your wife gave it to me."

"And where is this feather from?"

Hodjugur was silent. His brother shook him by the shoulders, he knew that some misfortune had occurred.

And Hodjugur began to cry.

"I found the skin by chance. Your wife asked me to let her hold it in her hands for a moment. Then she put it on and flew away. The cranes were calling her."

Yudjian had never struck his brother in anger. But now Hodjugur learned for the first time how terrible his brother's anger could be. Yudjian beat him with a heavy, braided whip, he called him a dog. At last, his anger quenched, he pushed Hodjugur away, ran to the stable, led out his finest horse, and mounted him. The reddish-golden horse, with a bright mane and tail, danced under him. Without a look at his brother, Yudjian rode out of the yard. But before he left, he picked up the white feather from the ground.

Yudjian galloped on the golden horse, the reins in one hand, the white feather in the other. The feather turned of itself, pointing the way.

It was a long ride. Yudjian crossed rivers, rode around lakes, tore through dense woods, galloped over plains. He slept under the open sky, shielded from the wind by the horse's wide back. He lost the count of days and nights.

At last he reached the foot of a high mountain. The feather rose, its sharp end pointing upward. Yudjian left his horse to graze in the green pasture and began to climb. The mountainside was steep. The first day Yudjian climbed only one quarter of the way. On the second day he reached the midpoint. Then, with renewed strength, for he saw a white yurt at the summit, he climbed on. The cliffs were ever steeper, ever more forbidding, the gorges ever wider, the rocks ever sharper. For yet another day he climbed and climbed, but in the end he reached the top and entered the white yurt.

Splendid skins covered the walls of the yurt. A merry fire gleamed in the fireplace. In the middle stood a golden cradle, and a Chichah-bird was rocking it. Seeing the man, the bird shook his wings and cried, "Cheep-chi-chip!" Then in a human voice he asked:

"Is your name Yudjian? Is it your wife you are searching for?"

"Yudjian is my name. And I am searching for my wife," he answered, his eyes never leaving the cradle.

"Well, then," said the bird, "come and look at your son."

Yudjian bent over the cradle and saw a beautiful child. The child stretched his arms to his father.

"Chee-chip!" said the bird. "The part seeks the whole, the little drop of blood longs for its own blood. Play with your child, Yudjian, I am tired of rocking the cradle."

Yudjian turned himself into a white ermine, ran up and down the cradle, jumped, and tumbled. And the boy laughed.

Light steps were heard, and the door creaked. The bird said:

"I do not know whether your wife will want to see you. Hide quickly!"

The ermine-Yudjian hid behind the skins. And the child began to cry without his playmate. A white crane ran into the yurt, threw off her skin, and the young mother hurried to the cradle. She took the child into her arms. He felt her warmth and grew quiet.

The ermine came out from behind the furs and turned back into Yudjian. He seized the feathered skin and threw it into the fire. The mother turned with a cry. Reproachfully, she whispered to her husband:

"Why, why did you do it?"

And she fell dead at his side.

Yudjian caught her in his arms, pressed her to his breast, tried to warm her with his breath, to bring her back to life. But the woman was motionless, sunk into the sleep of death. Yudjian laid her on the skins and bowed his head.

"This is my blackest day! My time of grief has come! She warned me, and I did not heed her warnings. I gave way to my violent heart, my hasty hand! She said misfortune would come of burning her skin - and now misfortune is here! I alone am to blame. I will redeem my guilt, I will make up for my rashness by patience and cunning. I will conquer weakness with strength, simplicity with guile. I will undo the harm I have done!"

Yudjian ran out of the yurt. A light cloud lingered near the mountaintop. He leaped upon it, and it floated away, swaying and billowing. They went on and on. The sun had set, the sky had darkened. The cloud swam along the great starry way. It came to a constellation and stood still.

Yudjian stepped off the cloud onto the Upper Earth. He looked around him. It was just as on the earth below-solid ground, a dwelling, a fire in the hearth.

On an eight-legged copper dais sat a young woman combing her red silken hair. Her hair was four times as long as her body, and she combed it with a golden comb and wrapped it on a silver staff. Yudjian said to her:

"Daughter of the Constellation, daughter of Master Yurgyal! Timid Shamaness Yurguk-Udagan! I have come to ask you to be my wife. Will you take me as your husband?"

The daughter of the Constellation looked at him. He was tall and handsome, and she answered quietly:

"I will."

"Then gather your clothes and your ornaments, and prepare for the journey. I shall await you on the top of the highest mountain."

The Timid Shamaness busied herself, preparing her clothes and her ornaments, gathering her dowry of cattle. And Yudjian went on.

He came to the yurt of the Master of the Moon. A young woman sat on an eight-legged copper dais, combing her silver-silk hair. Her hair was six times as long as her body, and she combed it with a golden comb, and wrapped it on a silver staff. Yudjian said to her:

"Daughter of the Master of the Moon, Shamaness of Moonlight! I have come to ask you to be my wife. Will you have me as your husband?"

The daughter of the Master of the Moon looked at him. His face shone with courage, his eyes were bright with spirit. And she said:

"I will. But give me time to get my dowry together."

"I have no time to wait," said Yudjian. "Do everything you need to do according to your own knowledge. Then come to me on the highest mountain. I shall await you there."

The daughter of the Master of the Moon, the Shamaness of Moonlight, busied herself, gathering her clothes and her adornments, calling together her dowry of cattle. And Yudjian went on.

While he walked, the night ended. In the distance gleamed the yurt of the Master of the Sun. Yudjian walked straight toward it.

Near the shining yurt, on an eight-legged copper dais sat a young woman, combing her sunny-silken hair. Her hair was eight times as long as her body, and she combed it with a golden comb, and wrapped it on a silver staff. Yudjian said to her:

"Daughter of the Master of the Sun! Shamaness Kugyal-Udagan! I have come to you to take you as my wife if you will have me as your husband!"

The Shamaness Kugyal-Udagan could look at the blazing face of her father, the Master of the Sun, without blinking. But now she shut her eyes, dazzled with love for him who had come to woo her. And she said to Yudjian:

"I will. Why not?"

Yudjian told her also to come to him on the highest mountain when she was ready.

The Shamaness Kugyal-Udagan remained to prepare her dowry, and Yudjian hastened on.

He came to the edge of the Upper Earth, leaped onto the cloud that was waiting for him, and started on his return journey. He floated up to the mountain and stepped off the cloud.

In the yurt the Chichah-bird rocked Yudjian's child, and on the furs lay Yudjian's dead wife. Yudjian quickly dressed her in his own clothes, gathered up her long hair and hid it under his hat. He brought her out of the yurt, laid her before the entrance, and hid behind the yurt.

Just as he finished, his three brides came riding on their horses from three directions. Each brought a rich dowry: dresses trimmed with braid, rare furs. Each had fifty herds of horses and ninety herds of cows. The whole mountainside was covered with the herds.

The brides dismounted and saw one another.

"Friends-sisters," they said, "so all three of us shall be the wives of the same husband. Well, we shall not be bored on Earth. But where is our husband? Why is he not here to welcome us? Let us go into the yurt. He may be sleeping."

They walked with cloud-light heavenly steps toward the yurt. Then suddenly they stopped: One said:

"Oh, my sisters! I fear there is a dead man lying here!"

The second one said:

"Can it be our husband?"

The third one looked:

"It is he! It is he! He came to woo me in these clothes!"

The daughter of the Master of the Sun, Kugyal-Udagan, asked:

"Daughter of Master Yurgyal, Timid Shamaness, can you re-vive a dead man?"

"If I said I can, it would be untrue. And if I said I cannot, it would be untrue," replied the Timid Shamaness. "I can revive a dead man so that he becomes as one lying unconscious."

"This is not much, and it is not little," said the daughter of the Master of the Sun. Then she asked the daughter of the Master of the Moon:

"And how great is your skill, Shamaness of Moonlight?"

"I can revive a dead man so that he becomes as one profoundly asleep," she answered.

"And I," said Kugyal-Udagan, daughter of the Master of the Sun, "can return a dead man to consciousness. I can awaken him from mortal sleep."

"Well, sisters!" said all three. "Let us do our work, let us bring our husband back to life."

The Timid Shamaness, daughter of the Constellation, was the first to leap across the body. Its breast stirred, its breath blew faintly from the lips.

The Shamaness of Moonlight was second to leap across the body. Color returned to the pale face, the eyelashes quivered.

And now Kugyal-Udagan, the daughter of the Master of the Sun, stepped forward. She leaped across the body, and the dead arose. The hat slipped down, and the long hair scattered on the shoulders.

"Oh, sisters, it seems we have revived the wrong one! This is not our husband, it is a strange woman!"

And Yudjian, who was hiding behind the yurt, had heard and seen everything. He ran out and embraced his beloved wife. She hid her face on his broad chest, flushing with joy.

The shamanesses watched and looked at one another. Suddenly the child cried in the yurt. The beautiful woman who had been brought to life heard it and broke away from her husband to run to her child. And Yudjian followed her.

"There is nothing for us to do here, sisters," said the daughter of the Master of the Sun. "Our bridegroom already has a wife and child. And it is not meant for us, heavenly shamanesses, to be junior wives, second to a woman of Earth! Let us return home."

She jumped upon her horse, the horse rose up and galloped straight into the sky. The two others followed her. On the way the daughter of Yurgyal, the Timid Shamaness, cried:

"Oh, sisters, what have we done? We have forgotten our dowries back on Earth!"

But Kugyal-Udagan, daughter of the Master of the Sun, laughed proudly.

"My father has more wealth than the few miserable herds I left below," she said. "He will not mind the loss. If I need more, he'll give me all I want."

"Nor will my father reproach me!" said the daughter of the Master of the Moon, the Shamaness of Moonlight.

Yurguk-Udagan, the daughter of the Constellation, flushed at these proud words.

"Let my dowry stay behind as well. My father, Master Yurgyal, is not as rich as yours, but he is as generous as they are. He too will not begrudge me anything."

And so they did not turn back. All the wealth, all three dowries, remained with Yudjian. He now prepared for the return journey. He whistled lightly, and his fiery horse came racing to him from the green valley below.

He mounted the horse, lifted up his wife before him, fastened his son's cradle at his left knee. On the edge of the cradle sat the faithful nurse, the Chichah-bird, singing songs to the boy.

Thrice fifty herds of horses ran before them. Thrice ninety herds of cows followed them.

This was how they journeyed, and this was how they came. A handsome youth, tall and broad in the shoulders, ran out to meet them.

"Is this you, Hodjugur, my younger brother?" asked Yudjian.

"Have I grown so much that you no longer recognize me?" laughed Hodjugur. "I see you found your wife, my dear sister-in-law, and brought her back. Forgive me for the trouble I have been to you!"

And they lived happily together. This is what people tell, this is what people sing about.

—Mirra Ginsburg
from *The Master of the Winds and Other Tales from Siberia*
A Yakut tale; the Yakuts are one of the largest
native groups in Siberia

Four Untitled Poems - #1

PARROTS DWELL IN THE WEST COUNTRY.
Foresters catch them with nets, to bring them to us.
Lovely women toy with them, morning and evening,
As they go to and from their courtyard pavilions.

They are given lordly gifts of golden cages—for their own
*   storage!*
Bolted in—their feathered coats are spoiled.
How unlike both swan and crane:
Wind-swirled and -tossed, they fly off into the clouds!

—Han Shan
from *Sunflower Splendor,*
Three Thousand Years of Chinese Poetry

The Man Who Dreamed of Fairies

THERE WAS ONCE A MAN who dreamt he went to Heaven:
His dream-body soared aloft through space.
He rode on the back of a white-plumed crane,
And was led on his flight by two crimson banners.
Whirring of wings and flapping of coat tails!
Jade bells suddenly all a-tinkle!
Half way to Heaven, he looked down beneath him,
Down on the dark turmoil of the World.
Gradually he lost the place of his native town;
Mountains and water—nothing else distinct.
The Eastern Ocean—a single strip of white:
The Hills of China—five specks of green.
Gliding past him a host of fairies swept
In long procession to the Palace of the Jade City.

—Po Chu-I
from *Translations from the Chinese*

Season of Cranes

THE SUN GLIMMERS RED IN THE WESTERN SKY
In the stillness slim reeds barely quiver
Flag-deer pause on the trail passing by
Wild turkeys roost in the trees while I
Sit still, oh so still, by the river

A chorus of plaintive trilling cries
Draws close and with wings quickly beating
The cranes that I watch for, multiply
From four winds they gather and darken the sky
New flocks steadfastly repeating

The coast in feet first, awkward acrobats
Whose numbers deft tabulation
Wings flapping, they settle into the Platte
Drawn by the gleam of the habitat
Seeking rest on springtime migration

In swaying ripples, on stilt-legs they stand
Sleek feathers of gray the same hue
As water they light in, this immigrant band
In the midst of the prairie, past hills built of sand
They fill the great Platte and renew

Just before dawn as air currents arise
And signal the proud birds their cue
Cranes lift glove-tipped wings and encompass the skies
Aloft in high breezes, long-limbed passers-by
Sail bleating toward northernmost views

A mandarin suns slips into the sky
In the stillness slim reeds barely quiver
Flag-deer drink at the shoreline nearby
Across the pasture a meadowlark flies...
Sweet calm reappears on the river

—Mary Beth Dodson
Written April 30, 1992

CRANE DANCING IN THE SKY.

—Robert H. van Gulik
from *The Lore of the Chinese Lute*

From *Thoughts in Early Autumn:*
Thirty Rhymes Sent to Lu-wang

ON CALM DAYS, I DRAW SPRING water with cupped hands;
When idle, pick up the milkweed to beat time with.
Junipers are nearly all short and scrubby,
Natural shallows form on the face of boulders.
Dwarf cassias sport leaves the size of fists;
New growth on pines, slender as fingertips.
The crying of cranes transmits the tones of the east,
Falcons swoop down with the twang of arrows.

—P'i Jih-hsiu
from *Sunflower Splendor,*
Three Thousand Years of Chinese Poetry

WHEN I LIE SLEEPLESS, LONGING FOR YAMATO,
Must you be so heartless, O cranes,
Crying around the end of the sand-bar?

—Osakabe Otomaro
from *The Manyosku: One Thousand Poems*

The Fox and the Crane

ONE DAY A FOX INVITED a crane to dinner, and since he
wanted to amuse himself at the expense of his guest, he
provided a meal that consisted only of some thin soup in a large
flat dish. The fox was able to lap this soup up very easily, while
the crane, unable to take a mouthful with her long narrow bill,
was as hungry at the end of dinner as when she began. Meanwhile, the fox pretended to regret seeing her eat so sparingly and
feared, so he said, that the dish might not be tasty enough for her.

The crane said little but requested the honor of allowing her to invite him to her place in the near future. He was delighted with the invitation, and a week later, he showed up punctually at the crane's home, where the dinner was served right away. To the fox's dismay, however, he found that the meal was contained in a narrow-necked vessel down which the crane easily thrust her long neck and bill, while he was obliged to content himself with licking the neck of the jar. Unable to satisfy his hunger, he left as graciously as possible, observing that he could hardly find fault with his host, who had only paid him back in his own coin.

Moral: Different people do different things well.

—Aesop's Fables

AS WE SEE STRANGE CRANES are wont to do
First stalk a while ere they their wings can find
Then soar from ground not past a yard or two,
Till in their wings they gathered have the wind;
At last they mount the very clouds unto
Trianglewise according to their kind.

—Lodovico Ariosto

From *The Toad*

This is a story about a toad looking for
"The Precious Stone" his mother told him about.

FROM THE TOP OF THE roof came the sound of the male stork clattering; he was giving a lecture to his family, but he kept his glance downward, for he was watching the two young men at the same time. "The human being is the most conceited of all the animals," he said. "Listen to them chattering; they should give their bills a rest. They pride themselves on their ability to speak, their linguistic ability! But if they travel as far as we do in a single day, they cannot comprehend one word that is spoken. They cannot understand each other, while we storks talk the same language all over the world, both in Egypt and in Denmark. As for flying, the human beings can't. When they want to move fast from one place to another, they have to use something called a railroad. It is an invention they will break their necks on. The very thought of it makes a chill run up and down my bill. The world can exist without them. We do not need human beings, all we need are frogs and worms."

"That was a great speech," thought the little toad. "The stork is a very important animal and it lives so high up, I have never seen anyone who lives higher!

"And look how it can swim!" the toad exclaimed out loud as the stork spread its wings and flew away through the air.

The female stayed in the nest and told the young ones about Egypt, about the waters of the great River Nile, and about all the remarkable mud to be found in foreign countries. It was all new and wonderful to the little toad.

"I must travel to Egypt," he said aloud. "I wonder if the stork or one of its young ones would take me. I would serve it faithfully all the rest of my days. Yes, I will get to Egypt, I am sure of it, for I am so happy. In me there is a longing and a desire that is sweet, and so much more valuable than any precious stone."

And that was the precious stone; and this was the toad who had it in his head: the eternal longing and desire for rising ever upward. That was the jewel! That was the flame that sparkled and shone with joy and desire.

At that moment the stork came. It had spied the little toad in the grass. Its bill did not grab it gently; it squeezed the toad. He was uncomfortable and frightened, yet he felt the wind blowing around him and knew that his course was upward toward Egypt; and therefore his eyes shone with expectation, as though a spark were flying from them.

"Croak!"

The heart stopped; the body was still, the toad was dead. But the spark that had shone in its eyes, what happened to that? The rays of the sun caught it, caught the gem that the little toad had carried in its head. But where did they take it?

Don't ask the scientist that question, ask the poet. He will tell you the answer, as a fable or a fairy tale. The caterpillar will be in his story, and the family of storks as well: The caterpillar changes itself into a beautiful butterfly. The stork flies over mountains and across oceans to distant Africa, and returns by the shortest route to Denmark—to that particular place, to that particular house where his nest is. That, too, is magic and unexplainable, and yet it happens. You may ask the scientist, he has to admit it; and you yourself know it is true, for you have seen it.

But what about the gem in the toad's head?

Seek it in the sun, see if you can find it there!

No, the light is too intense; we do not yet have eyes that can see all the glory God has created. But maybe someday we will have such eyes. That will be the most wonderful fairy tale of all, for we ourselves will be part of it.

—Hans Christian Andersen
Written 1866

COOL SEASCAPE WITH CRANES
    Wading long-legged in the pools
      Mid the Tideway dunes.

—Basho
From *Tales Alive! Bird Tales from Near & Far*

Seeing Meng Haoran off to Yangzhou From Yellow Crane Tower

AT YELLOW CRANE TOWER IN THE WEST
My old friend says farewell;
In the mist and flowers of spring
He goes down to Yangzhou;
Lonely sail, distant shadow,
Vanish in blue emptiness;
All I see is the great river
Flowing into the far horizon.

—Li Bai
from *Poetry and Prose of the Tang and Song*

SHALL I NOT MISS THE DAINTY SEAWEED
On the rugged island beach
When it is hidden under the flood tide?
As the tide flows into Waka Bay,
The cranes, with the lagoons lost in flood,
Go crying towards the reedy shore.

—Yamabe Akahito
Early to Middle Nara period
from *The Manyosku: One Thousand Poems*
Poem compares the association of cranes
with the beauties of nature.

Wonder of Cranes
Will Perpetuate
Through the Centuries

I KNEW IT WOULD BE difficult to top last year.

Last year, besides all the birds, we saw a full moon, a comet and lots of deer. The year before, we saw a couple beavers frolic in a nearby pond.

This year, as we drove to our bunker, we viewed a skunk ambling in a field. We were told of resident raccoons and a badger dig nearby. There were deer again, off to the west in the same field.

And, of course, there was the featured attraction—the thousands and thousands of waterfowl and cranes, gracing the skies as the sun vanished over the horizon.

As the geese first, and then the cranes began to circle and fill the darkening skies, I remembered that this was a ceremony of nature dating back millions of years.

A half-century ago, in 1948, songs of Nat King Cole and the Andrews Sisters lit up the airwaves. Back then, too, the song of the sandhill crane lit up this valley for miles around.

It was on this day in 1852, shortly before the Civil War, when Harriet Beecher Stowe's classic book, *Uncle Tom's Cabin,* was published. That year, the classic migration of the sandhill crane proceeded, as usual.

On this day, exactly five centuries ago, Christopher Columbus was planning his third voyage to the Americas. He didn't know about it, but at that time sandhill cranes were migrating through the heart of this unexplored continent.

On this day, five centuries before Columbus, a man called Eric the Red had already discovered Iceland and Greenland. But his son, Leif Ericson would sail to North America three years later. Every March of every year that these two famed Norwegian explorers sailed the high Atlantic seas, an amazing gathering of cranes was taking place thousands of miles away.

Indeed, two millennia ago, around the year 1 BC, Jesus Christ was growing up a young boy in a holy land. In another land far, far way, masses of sandhill cranes were stopping amid a migration noticed only by their counterparts in the natural world.

Another five hundred years prior to that—2,500 years ago—a person named Confucius was alive and earning fame as a man of learning and character. Even way back then, halfway around the world, multitudes of sandhill cranes were taking a breather from their migration.

There is something reassuring about the natural world, about the synchronicity of nature, about the changing of the seasons and the everlasting beckoning of the outdoors. There is something incredibly comforting in knowing that this journey, by these birds, will perpetuate.

As we left, the cranes' cries pierced every corner of the sky. It was the first really nice day in weeks, our guide said, so the cranes were probably celebrating by having a little fun. It was well past sunset, but they continued to circle the river—almost like a show of strength, a show of amazing persistence.

We will return here again next year, as will the cranes. This rite of nature will persevere long after we are gone.

Someday, it is certain, our grandchildren and great grandchildren and, yes, even our descendents centuries down the road, will return to this same place and view this same marvelous site.

—Pete Letheby
The Grand Island Independent

Part Three

Going Alone to Spend a Night At the Hsien-yu Temple

THE CRANE FROM THE SHORE standing at the top of the steps;
The moon on the pool seen at the open door;
Where these are, I made my lodging-place
And for two nights could not turn away.
I am glad I chanced on a place so lonely and still
With no companion to drag me early home.
Now that I have tasted the joy of being alone
I will never again come with a friend at my side.

—Po Chu-I
from *Translations from the Chinese*

From *The Enchanted Bluff*

WE HAD OUR SWIM BEFORE sundown, and while we were cooking our supper the oblique rays of light made a dazzling glare on the white sand about us. The translucent red ball itself sank behind the brown stretches of corn field as we sat down to eat, and the warm layer of air that had rested over the water and our clean sand bar grew fresher and smelled of the rank iron-weed and sunflowers growing on the flatter shore. The river was brown and sluggish, like any other of the half-dozen streams that water the Nebraska corn lands. On one shore was an irregular line of bald clay bluffs where a few scrub oaks with thick trunks and flat, twisted tops threw light shadows on the long grass. The western shore was low and level, with corn fields that stretched to the skyline, and all along the water's edge were little sandy coves and beaches where slim cottonwoods and willow saplings flickered.

Suddenly we heard a scream above our fire, and jumped up to see a dark, slim bird floating southward far above us—a whooping crane, we knew by her cry and her long neck. We ran to the edge of the island, hoping we might see her alight, but she wavered southward along the river course until we lost her.

—Willa Cather
abbreviated from *The Enchanted Bluff*

Crane Watching

HE SITS HUNCHED IN HIS OLD BLACK COAT
on the railroad, staring through the ties
at the Platte below and remembers,
as a child, watching gravel pour from a truck
and catching one stone with his eyes
and tracing it to bedrock.

The people gathering on the bridge at dusk
to watch the cranes come in
give him berth,
not so wide as for the homeless
whose eyes are fixed on a vanishing point
but a respectful one,
for they too will forget themselves shortly,
faces raised,
trying to put a finger on millennia.
—Anne Meredith McCollister

From *On the Lake near the Western Mountains*

THE ATMOSPHERE WITH NIGHTFALL GROWETH CLEARER
A north wind blows with shrill voice through
the land;
While on the sandy stretches by the waters
The swan and stork in dreamy silence stand.
—Ch'ang Kien
T'ang Dynasty (ancient style)
from *Chinese Poems*
translated by Charles Budd—printed 1912
with permission of Oxford University Press

Wisconsin—Marshland Elegy

A DAWN WIND STIRS ON the great marsh. With almost imperceptible slowness it rolls on bank of fog across the wide morass. Like the white ghost of a glacier the mists advance, riding over phalanxes of tamarack, sliding across bog-meadows heavy with dew. A single silence hangs from horizon to horizon.

Out of some far recess of the sky a tinkling of little bells falls soft upon the listening land. Then again silence. Now comes a baying of some sweet-throated hound, soon the clamor of a responding pack. Then a far clear blast of hunting horns, out of the sky into the fog.

High horns, low horns, silence, and finally a pandemonium of trumpets, rattles, croaks, and cries that almost shakes the bog with its nearness, but without yet disclosing whence it comes. At last a glint of sun reveals the approach of the great echelon of birds. On motionless wing they emerge from the lifting mists, sweep a final arc of sky, and settle in clangorous descending spirals to their feeding grounds. A new day has begun on the crane marsh.

A sense of time lies thick and heavy on such a place. Yearly since the ice age it has awakened each spring to the clangor of cranes. The peat layers that comprise the bog are laid down in the basin of an ancient lake. The cranes stand, as it were, upon the sodden pages of their own history. These peats are the compressed remains of the mosses that clogged the pools, of the tamaracks that spread over the moss, of the cranes that bugled over the tamaracks since the retreat of the ice sheet. An endless caravan of generations has built of its own bones this bridge into the future, this habitat where the oncoming host again may live and breed and die.

To what end? Out on the bog a crane, gulping some luckless frog, springs his ungainly hulk into the air and flails the morning sun with mighty wings. The tamaracks re-echo with his bugled certitude. He seems to know.

Our ability to perceive quality in nature begins, as in art, with the pretty. It expands through successive stages of the beautiful to values as yet uncaptured by language. The quality of cranes lies, I think, in this higher gamut, as yet beyond the reach of words.

This much, though, can be said: our appreciation of the crane grows with the slow unraveling of earthly history. His tribe, we now know, stems out of the remote Eocene. The other members of the fauna in which he originated are long since entombed within the hills. When we hear his call we hear no mere bird. We hear the trumpet in the orchestra of evolution. He is the symbol of our untamable past, of that incredible sweep of millennia which underlies and conditions the daily affairs of birds and men.

And so they live and have their being – these cranes – not in the constricted present, but in the wider reaches of evolutionary time. Their annual return is the ticking of the geologic clock. Upon the place of their return they confer a peculiar distinction. Amid the endless mediocrity of the commonplace, a crane marsh holds a paleontological patent of nobility, won in the march of aeons, and revocable only by shotgun. The sadness discernible in some marshes arises, perhaps, from their once having harbored cranes. Now they stand humbled, adrift in history.

Some sense of this quality in cranes seems to have been felt by sportsmen and ornithologists of all ages. Upon such quarry as this the Holy Roman Emperor Frederick loosed his gyrfalcons. Upon such quarry as this one swooped the hawks of Kublai Khan. Marco Polo tells us; 'He derives the highest amusement from sporting with gyrfalcons and hawks. At Changanor the Khan has a great Palace surrounded by a fine plain where are found cranes in great numbers. He causes millet and other grains to be sown in order that the birds may not want.'

The ornithologist Bengt Berg, seeing cranes as a boy upon the Swedish heaths, forthwith made them his life work. He followed them to Africa and discovered their winter retreat on the White Nile. He says of his first encounter: 'It was a spectacle which eclipsed the flight of the roc in the Thousand and One Nights.'

When the glacier came down out of the north, crunching hills and gouging valleys, some adventuring rampart of the ice climbed the Baraboo Hills and fell back into the outlet gorge of the Wisconsin River. The swollen waters backed up and formed a lake half as long as the state, bordered on the east by cliffs of ice, and fed by the torrents that fell from melting mountains. The shorelines of this old lake are still visible; its bottom is the bottom of the great marsh.

The lake rose through the centuries, finally spilling over east of the Baraboo range. There it cut a new channel for the river, and thus drained itself. To the residual lagoons came the cranes, bugling the defeat of the retreating winter, summoning the on-creeping host of living things to their collective task of marsh-building. Floating bogs of sphagnum moss clogged the lowered waters, filled them. Sedge and leatherleaf, tamarack and spruce successively advanced over the bog, anchoring it by their root fabric, sucking out its water, making peat. The lagoons disappeared, but not the cranes. To the moss-meadows that replace the ancient waterways they returned each spring to dance and bugle and rear their gangling sorrel-colored young. These, albeit birds, are not properly called chicks, but colts. I cannot explain why. On some dewy June morning watch them gambol over their ancestral pastures at the heels of the roan mare, and you will see for yourself.

One year not long ago a French trapper in buckskins pushed his canoe up one of the moss-clogged creeks that thread the great marsh. At this attempt to invade their miry stronghold the cranes gave vent to loud and ribald laughter. A century or two later Englishmen came in covered wagons. They chopped clearings in the timbered moraines that border the marsh, and in them planted corn and buckwheat. They did not intend, like the Great Khan at Changanor, to feed the cranes. But the cranes do not question the intent of glaciers, emperors, or pioneers. They ate the grain, and when some irate farmer failed to concede their usufruct in his corn, they trumpeted a warning and sailed across the marsh to another farm.

There was no alfalfa in those days, and the hill-farms made poor hay land, especially in dry years. One dry year someone set a fire in the tamaracks. The burn grew up quickly to bluejoint grass, which, when cleared of dead trees, made a dependable hay meadow. After that, each August, men appeared to cut hay. In winter, after the cranes had gone South, they drove wagons over the frozen bogs and hauled the hay to their farms in the hills. Yearly they plied the marsh with fire and axe, and in two short decades hay meadows dotted the whole expanse.

Each August when the haymakers came to pitch their camps, singing and drinking and lashing their teams with whip and tongue, the cranes whinnied to their colts and retreated to the far fastnesses. 'Red shitepokes' the haymakers called them, from the rusty hue which at that season often stains the battleship-gray of crane plumage. After the hay was stacked and the marsh again their own, the cranes returned, to call down out of October skies the migrant flocks from Canada. Together they wheeled over the new-cut stubbles and raided the corn until frosts gave the signal for the winter exodus.

These haymeadow days were the Arcadian age for marsh dwellers. Man and beast, plant and soil lived on and with each other in mutual toleration, to the mutual benefit of all. The marsh might have kept on producing hay and prairie chickens, deer and muskrat, crane-music and cranberries forever.

The new overlords did not understand this. They did not in-clude soil, plants, or birds in their ideas of mutuality. The dividends of such a balanced economy were too modest. They envisaged farms not only around, but in the marsh. An epidemic of ditch-digging and land-booming set in. The marsh was gridironed with drainage canals, speckled with new fields and farmsteads.

But crops were poor and beset by frosts, to which the expensive ditches added an aftermath of debt. Farmers moved out. Peat beds dried, shrank, caught fire. Sun-energy out of the Pleistocene shrouded the countryside in acrid smoke. No man raised his voice against the waste, only his nose against the smell. After a dry summer not even the winter snows could extinguish the smoldering marsh. Great pockmarks were burned into field and meadow, the scars reaching down to the sands of the old lake, peat-covered these hundred centuries. Rank weeds sprang out of the ashes, to be followed after a year or two by aspen scrub. The cranes were hard put, their numbers shrinking with the remnants of unburned meadow. For them, the song of the power shovel came near being an elegy. The high priests of progress knew nothing of cranes, and cared less. What is a species more or less among engineers? What good is an undrained marsh anyhow?

For a decade or two crops grew poorer, fires deeper, woodfields larger, and cranes scarcer, year by year. Only reflooding, it appeared, could keep the peat from burning. Meanwhile cranberry growers had, by plugging drainage ditches, reflooded a few spots and obtained good yields. Distant politicians bugled about marginal land, over production, unemployment relief, conservation. Economists and planners came to look at the marsh. Surveyors, technicians, CCCs, buzzed about. A counter-epidemic of reflooding set in. Government bought land, resettled farmers, plugged ditches wholesale. Slowly the bogs are re-wetting. The fire-pocks became ponds. Grass fires still burn, but they can no longer burn the wetted soil.

All this, once the CCC camps were gone, was good for cranes, but not so the thickets of scrub popple that spread inexorably over the old burns, and still less the maze of new roads that inevitably follow governmental conservation. To build a road is so much simpler than to think of what the country really needs. A roadless marsh is seemingly as worthless to the alphabetical conservationist as an undrained one was to the empire-builders. Solitude, the one natural resource still undowered of alphabets, is so far recognized as valuable only by ornithologists and cranes.

Thus always does history, whether of marsh or market place, end in paradox. The ultimate value in these marshes is wildness, and the crane is wildness incarnate. But all conservation of wildness is self-defeating, for to cherish we must see and fondle, and when enough have seen and fondled, there is no wilderness left to cherish.

Some day, perhaps in the very process of our benefactions, perhaps in the fullness of geologic time, the last crane will trumpet his farewell and spiral skyward from the great marsh. High out of the clouds will fall the sound of hunting horns, the baying of the phantom pack, the tinkle of little bells, and then a silence never to be broken, unless perchance in some far pasture of the Milky Way.

—Aldo Leopold
from *A Sand County Almanac and Sketches Here and There*
Copyright 1949
with permission of Oxford University Press

The Long Gray Line

A LONG FRAGILE FILAMENT, CONNECTED TO A
Past obscured by time and evolution
That time of mastodon giants, shadows of
All dimensions, now obscure in resolution
Most of those shadows have since turned to stone
And we know them only by images cast for time,
One can only imagine a primal scene
To match these footprints and images so sublime
That is until we hear that mystic sound from the sky,
The bugle of this connecting filament from our past
At closer observation, one sees an awesome image
Cranes gliding in the sky and maybe understands at last

The sound, the sight, the wonder of it all
Come together like a season's change
And bring the here and now into sharper focus
As one-half million images come into range
The body senses tell us with strong authority
That this is something special coming to our view
And that the Creator of this lifeline to the past
Offers another chance, our spirit to renew

The stay is oh so short, and the time does come
When a southerly breeze beckons them go
And a thawing tundra offers respite for awhile
Until the egg has hatched and sky threatens snow
And that line goes again towards a southward sky
And a few may notice the gray filament passing by
Faith alone will sustain us now, in the days ahead
'Til those days in spring when this ancient thread
Will again grace our eye....

—Ward Schrack
Spring 1995

Rowe Sanctuary

THIS SANCTUARY KNOWS ITS PLACE.
It has so for a million years,
its grasses the original transcriptions
of how sterns whisper wind.

And no one interprets this river
better than the cranes,
each one a long gray syllable
in the book of love.

This sanctuary says, Come in.
Wash your faces in the wind,
co-create wonder with your eyes,
treat your soles to something
other than cement.

Worship is a natural event.
It's here you justify your lives.

—Dr. Don Welch
for Rowe Sanctuary's 25th Anniversary

Psalm 104, Verse 16 and 17

THE TREES OF THE LORD ARE WELL WATERED,
the cedars of Lebanon that he planted.

There the birds make their nests;
the stork has her home in the fir trees.

—Holy Bible, New King James Version

A Slight Error

T HE RABBIT CAME HURRYING to the Crane's office. "Dear Doctor Crane," he said, "you're good at fixing teeth. Please give me some new ones!"

"But your teeth are fine!"

"They may be fine, but they're too short. Please fix me up with some long teeth like the Lion's!"

"Why do you want long teeth?"

"Because I want to settle accounts with the Fox. I'm tired of always running away from him! Let him run away from me for a change!"

Dr. Crane smiled, and then proceeded to outfit the Rabbit with false teeth – two long lion's fangs. They were just like real! Frightful to see!

"Marvelous!" said the Rabbit, looking at himself in the mirror. "Now I'll go looking for the Fox!"

He went dashing off through the woods, and almost before he knew it, the Fox himself leaped at him from behind a bush.

The Rabbit jumped backward, spun around, and took off as fast as his legs could carry him.

He ran back to Dr. Crane, shaking and trembling with fright. "Please, Doctor," he begged, "give me some new fangs!"

"What's wrong with the ones I gave you?"

"Nothing, except they're too short. They're not what I need for the Fox. Do you have any longer ones?"

"I'm sorry, Peter my boy," said Dr. Crane, "but I really can't help you. I made a slight error. I should have given you a lion's heart instead of lion's teeth."

—Sergei Makhalkov
from *Let's Fight!: And other Russian Fables*

110

Perfect Crane

N O ONE CAN HOLD THE wind, or catch the sun, or spin the world like a magician. Some are more powerful than others and some are kinder than others, but none was ever more blessed with magic than Gami.

In painted sandals and printed robes he walked the streets of his town, never speaking to anyone, for he was sure only magicians were interested in magic. And the townsfolk, not knowing what a magician does, never wanted to trouble him. Yet inside, Gami was always troubled.

Alone in his house Gami practiced his magic during the day, chanting his charms and spells. But at night he sat silently without a friend to laugh with him or a neighbor to talk to him. Gami's only companions were his hands, busy folding brightly colored paper into flowers and fish and faces. Butterflies of bright blues and reds covered his walls, and delicate birds danced on string in his windows. Gami gave them all his love, for there was no one else.

One dark night Gami folded a speckled red paper into a lily. "Bright flower," he said, "won't you bloom for me and cheer this dreary night?" And then, because Gami *was* a magician, the tiny flower opened its petals right in his hand. Gami was astonished.

He had worked much magic, but he had never breathed life into his paper before. He was truly pleased.

The following night Gami folded a lantern of heavy green paper. "Lovely lantern," Gami said, "won't you glow and brighten my tiny house?" And then, because Gami *was* a magician, the lantern dazzled. Gami was so delighted that he did not sleep all night.

When the day came Gami went directly to the market and bought the finest rice paper, in the purest white. He rolled it carefully and slipped it up his sleeve for safekeeping. Gami had special plans.

That night Gami unrolled his purest-white paper and began folding a crane. He had folded cranes before, with upward wings and lowered heads, but this crane had to be the most perfect. He spent many hours carefully creasing the paper, until at last he set the finished paper bird on the floor.

Gami admired the bird and thought it was the most beautiful he had ever seen. And beyond a doubt, it was. "I have made a flower bloom and a lantern glow," said Gami. "Perfect crane, won't you too come to life for me so I will not be alone anymore?"

Slowly the crane rose off the floor and flew up until it was no longer made of paper. It was a real crane. Gami held out his arm and the crane landed gently on it. "You are my father," the crane said. "You have given me life and I am grateful." Gami was filled with joy, knowing he would never be alone again.

Every day Gami and his crane traveled the town. People looked out of their windows and stopped what they were doing to stare, and soon they could no long keep quiet.

"Where did you find such a bird?" one man called out to Gami. "For I have truly seen no other like it."

"There *is* no other like it," Gami answered.

"Magician," a woman asked, "how do you get such a bird to follow you, to live in your house?"

"With my magic," answered Gami. He smiled and would say no more.

"Curious, that magician," his neighbors said. "He is cleverer than we ever guessed." And they came to Gami's house one by one to see the bird and to speak with the magician. The crane gracefully balanced on one leg as Gami talked and joked with his neighbors through the hours of the days.

Then after many months, when the sunlight began to grow weaker and the breeze colder, the crane perched on Gami's windowsill and said, "It is time for me to go."

"What do you mean?" Gami asked. "We have nowhere to go."

"I must join a flock and fly to follow the sun. It is time," said the crane.

"You have given me happiness," Gami said quickly. "Together we have found our friends around us. You cannot leave me."

"You have given me life," the crane said, "but I cannot stay."

Gami lowered his head and began to cry. "I made you," he said, "and now you are going to leave me alone again. I will make you stay."

"Then you will have to return me to paper," the crane said. "A paper bird does not fly and does not need to follow the sun. But a real bird must. There is no other way."

Gami looked at the perfect white crane. He did not want a paper bird and he did not want his perfect crane to fly away.

"Father," the crane said, "I will return in the spring with many stories to tell you. And you will have much to tell me."

Gami was silent. He did not think he would have much to tell if the crane left him. But he knew he had no choice. He had to let his crane go.

And yet, after the crane had joined a flock and flown away, Gami was not left alone. His neighbors, who had first come to see the bird, still came to be with him. They shared their meals and warmed the chilly winter hours with friendly talk. Gami listened to his neighbors, and with his magic he would help if he could. Soon his days and nights were filled with the puzzles and problems of this friend or that.

"Seek the magician," people now said to one another, "whenever you need a friend." And Gami was always glad to lend a hand or a heart.

For many months Gami was so busy that he did not notice the small sprigs of grass or the buds on the trees. He did not notice spring.

Then one day as the new sun filled Gami's house, a shadow crossed his window and he looked up to see the perfect crane land on the sill. Gami rushed to the window, and when he reached the crane he stopped and bowed his head in thanks.

"You have returned," Gami said at last.

"As I always will," the crane answered. "And I have so much to tell you." The crane described a faraway port where small boats bob on salty green water. "I have spent nights by swiftly running rivers and found harvested winter fields with loose grain to eat. I have come to know many places, Father."

"That is good," said Gami. "I have come to know many people. Old Miki down the hill lost all his chickens save one. I shed a spell on her so that every egg she lays is twins." Gami smiled with delight and the crane nodded his head in approval.

"And surely you remember that small boy, that sick boy who can only sit in a chair at his door. For him," Gami said proudly, "I folded out of fine sturdy paper a kite without string, a bird without wings. It is a toy never seen before that he sails through the air and that always returns to land in his lap. Children gather from all around to watch, but the toy works only or him. I was surely pleased with that!"

"Come, there is much to show you," Gami said, and together they went out into the streets of the town. People stopped them to greet the bird and to give thanks that he had returned to their friend. And some people stopped them just because they needed Gami's help, for now everyone knew the good work of the magician.

While the blossoms on the trees turned to fruit in the sun, Gami and his crane spent long days in the streets and the markets and the houses of good friends.

—Anne Laurin

The Word Crane in Other Languages

Kurrile	Albanian
Yashtahi	Arabic
Jerab	Czech
Trane	Danish
Kraan or Hijskraan	Dutch
Lev'masino	Esperanto, artificial European language
Nosturi	Finnish
Grue	French
Kran	German and Polish
Yeranos'	Greek
Manof	Hebrew
Daru	Hungarian
Mesin derek-derek or Burung bangau	Indonesian
Gru	Italian
Kijuuki	Japanese
Cucu-wa-njoka	Kikuyu, a tribe in Kenya
Nakandunga	Kwanyama, in southeast China
Heisekran	Norwegian
Gahaquaront (heron)	Onondaga, Indian tribe who inhabited New York
Peto	Osage, Indian tribe of Ohio Valley and western Missouri
Peto xodse (gray crane)	Osage, Indian tribe of Ohio Valley and western Missouri
Peto hiustse dse (sandhill crane)	Osage, Indian tribe of Ohio Valley and western Missouri
Peto cka (white crane)	Osage, Indian tribe of Ohio Valley and western Missouri
Kalank	Persian
Guindaste or Grou	Portuguese

Macara	Romanian
Kypabjib or Kran	Russian
Dizalica or Zdral	Serbo-Croatian
Zerjav	Slovene, in eastern Czechoslovakia
Grulla	Spanish
Winchi	Swahili, in east Africa
Lyftkran	Swedish
Tagak (heron)	Tagalog, national language of the Pilipino
Vinc	Turkish
Cai truc hang	Vietnamese
Oifheiber	Yiddish

Peiter, Peter, and Peer

IT IS UNBELIEVABLE HOW MUCH children in our age know. Why, one hardly knows what they don't know. That the stork has brought them from the well or the millpond and delivered them to their father and mother is such an old story that they don't believe it; and that is too bad, for it is the truth.

But how do the little babies get in the millpond or the well? That is something not everybody knows, yet there are some who do. Have you ever looked at the heavens on a clear night when all the stars are out? Then you will have noticed the shooting stars. They look as if they were falling and then suddenly they disappear. The most learned cannot explain what they don't understand themselves; but if you know, then you can, even if you are not learned. What looks like a little Christmas-tree candle falling from the heavens is the spark of a soul coming from God. It flies down toward the earth. As it comes into our heavy atmosphere, its glow becomes so faint that our eyes can no longer see it. It is so fine and fragile, it is a little child of the heavens, a little angel; but without wings, for it will be a human being. Slowly, it glides through the air, and the wind carries it and puts it down inside a flower. It may be a violet, a rose, or a carnation. There it lies for a while. It is so tiny and airy that a fly—or a bee—could fly away with it.

When the fly and the bee come to search for honey, the little air-child is in the way; but they don't kick it out, they are too kind for that; no, they carry it to a water-lily leaf and leave it there. The air-children climb down into the water, where they sleep and grow until they have reached the right size. Then, when the stork thinks one of them is big enough, he picks it up and flies with it to a family who want a sweet little child. But whether the children are sweet or not, depends upon what they have drunk while they lay in the millpond; whether they have drunk clear water, or water filled with mud and duckweed, for that makes the airchild very earthy.

The stork never tries to do any matching up, he thinks that the first place is the best. One baby comes to wonderful parents, another to a mother and father so hard and mean that it would have been better to stay in the millpond.

The little ones cannot remember what they have dreamed while they lay under the water lilies and the frogs sang for them, "Croak . . . croak . . . croak!" That, in human language, means: "Come sleep and dream." They have no memory either of which flower they have lain in or what it smelled like, though sometimes when they grow up, something inside them will say, "I like that flower best." And that is the flower they slept in when they were air-children.

The stork lives to be very old, and he always takes an interest in the children he has brought and how they fare in this world. He can't do anything for them, he can't change their circumstances, for he has his own family to look after. But he doesn't forget them; on the contrary, he thinks about them often.

I know an old stork, a very honorable bird, who is very learned. He has delivered a lot of children and knows the story of them all. There isn't a one that doesn't have a bit of duckweed and mud in it. I asked him to tell the biography of just one child, and he gave me three for the one I asked for. They all had the same family name: Peitersen.

Now the family Peitersen was very respectable. The husband was one of the town's two-and-thirty councilors, and that was a great distinction, so he devoted his whole life to being a councilor, and that was what he lived for. Now first the stork brought them a little Peiter; that was the name they gave the child. And the next year he came with another boy, and they called him Peter. And the third year Peer was brought. Peiter, Peter, and Peer—all variations of the same name: Peitersen.

They were three brothers, three shooting stars. Each had lain in a flower and slept beneath the leaf of a water lily in the millpond, and from there they had been brought by the stork to the family Peitersen who lived in the house on the corner; and everyone in town knew whose house it was.

They grew in body and spirit, and all three wanted to be something finer than one of the town's two-and-thirty men.

Peiter said he wanted to be a robber, but that was because he had seen the comedy, *Fra Diavolo,* which had convinced him that a robber's trade was the best in the world. Peter wanted to be a trumpet player. And Peer, that sweet little well-behaved child, so plump and round, whose only fault was that he bit his nails, he wanted to be a "daddy." These were the answers they gave when anyone asked them what they wanted to be when they grew up.

They were sent to school, and one was the head of the class; another in the middle; and the third was the dunce, which doesn't mean that they weren't equally clever and good. Their parents, who had insight, swore that they were. The boys attended their first children's ball, smoked cigars when no one was looking, and generally became cleverer and more educated.

Peiter was the most difficult, which is not unusual for a r ber. He was, in truth, a very naughty child; but that was caused, according to his mother, by worms. Naughty children always suffer from worms, they have mud in their stomachs. Once his stubbornness and obstinacy brought about the ruin of his mother's new silk dress.

"Don't shake the coffee table, my God's lamb," she had said. "You might upset the cream pitcher and splash my new silk dress."

119

The God's lamb grabbed the handle of the cream pitcher and poured its contents right down in Mama's lap. The poor woman could not help saying, "My lamb, my little lamb, how could you do such a thing?" That the child had a will of his own she had no doubt. A will of one's own is the same as character; and that to a mother is a sign of great promise.

He could have become a robber but he didn't; he only dressed like one. He wore an old hat and let his hair grow. He was going to be an artist, but he never got any further than dressing like one. More than anything else, he looked like a bedraggled hollyhock. As a matter of fact, he drew all his models so terribly tall that they looked like hollyhocks. It was the flower he loved best of all; the stork said that he had once lain in one.

Peter had lain in a buttercup, and he looked greasy around the corner of his mouth. His skin was so yellow that, if he was cut in his cheek, I am sure butter would have oozed out. He was born to sell butter, and could have had his own shop with a sign about it, except that, deep inside himself, he was a trumpet player. He was the musical member of the Peitersen family, and that single one was noisy enough for them all, said the neighbors. He composed seventeen polkas in one week and then transcribed them into an opera for trumpet and drums. Ugh! Was it lovely!

Peer was white and pink, little and ordinary; he had lain in a daisy. He didn't fight back when the older boys hit him; he was sensible, and the sensible person always gives up. When he was very small he collected slate pencils; later he collected stamps; and finally he was given a little cabinet to keep a zoological collection in. He had a dried fish, three newborn blind rats in alcohol, and a stuffed mole. Peer was a scientist and a naturalist. His parents were very proud of him and Peer was very proud of himself. He preferred a walk in the forest to going to school. Nature attracted him more than education.

Both his brothers were engaged, while Peer was still dedicating his life to completing his collection of the eggs of web-footed birds. He knew a great deal more about animals than he did about human beings. As for the highest feeling, love, he was of the opinion that man was inferior to the animal. He knew that the male nightingale would serenade his wife the whole night through, while she was sitting on the eggs. He—Peer—could never have done that; nor could he, like the stork, have stood on one leg on top of the roof all night, just to guard his wife and family; he couldn't have stood there an hour.

One day, as he was studying a spider and its web, he gave up the idea of marrying altogether. Mr. Spider weaves his nets to catch thoughtless flies, young or old, fat or thin; he exists only to weave nets and support his family. But Mrs. Spider has only one thought in her mind: her husband. She eats him up, out of love. She eats his head, his heart, and his body; only the long thin legs are left dangling in the web, where he used to sit worrying about the family. This is the truth, taken right out of a zoology book. Peer saw it, and thought about it. "To be so adored by one's wife that she eats one up—no human being can love like that, and maybe it's just as well."

Peer decided never to get married and never to give any girl a kiss, for that is the first step toward marriage. But he got a kiss, the kiss none of us escapes, the final kiss of death. When we have lived long enough, the order is given to Death: "Kiss away!" and away we go. A light comes from God, so bright that it blinds us and everything grows dark. The human soul that came as a falling star flies away again, but not to rest in a flower or dream beneath the water-lily leaf. Now its journey is more important; it flies into eternity and what that is like, no one knows. No one has seen that far, not even the stork, however good his eyesight is, and however much he knows.

He didn't know any more about Peer, but a great deal more about Peiter and Peter. I had heard enough about them, and I am sure you have too, I said thank you to the bird. And imagine, for such an ordinary story, the stork wanted payment. He wanted it in kind: three frogs and one young grass snake. Will you pay him? I won't! I have neither frogs nor young grass snakes on me.

—Hans Christian Andersen
Written 1868
translated by Henrietta Nygaard Rasmussen

The Farmer and the Cranes

SOME CRANES SETTLED DOWN in a farmer's field that had recently been sown with wheat and made it their feeding grounds. For some time the farmer frightened them away by threatening them with an empty sling. But when the cranes discovered that he was only slinging air, they were no longer afraid of him and would not fly away. Consequently, the farmer slung stones and killed a good number of the birds. In response the rest of the cranes took off and cried out to each other, "It's time for us to be off. This man isn't just threatening us any longer. He's really serious about getting rid of us."

Moral: If words do not suffice, blows must follow.

—Aesop's Fables

WHEN CRANES COME HITHER tis Spring and sowing time.
They feed on grain uncovered which they find.

—Monk Mantuan
born 1448

Bittersweet is the Crane

IN YOU, I SEE IMAGES OF OTHER TIMES ... days long past ...
Keeping your appointment with destiny ...
I wonder if you know ...

Your dignity is serene ... you transport joy and beauty
into my heart ...

I am of no importance to you ... you are immeasurably
moving to my soul ...

Your hearts are open to love ... you mourn for one lost
and left behind ...

I think you are lonely for home, while on your timeless
journey ...

The spring seasons of my life are more beautiful, because of
you ...

The welcoming arms of the Great Platte River will be open
always to you ... to those who will come after you ...
thru the aeons of time ...

There will be countless privileged mortals encountering in you,
God's magnificent creation.

—Gerry Sheperd

123

WE WERE LYING FLAT ON our backs, soaking up November sun, staring idly at a soaring buzzard overhead. Far beyond him the sky suddenly exhibited a rotating circle of white spots, alternately visible and invisible. A faint bugle not soon told us they were cranes, inspecting their Delta and finding it good. At the time my ornithology was homemade, and I was pleased to think them whooping cranes because they were so white. Doubtless they were sandhill cranes, but it doesn't matter. What matters is that we were sharing our wilderness with the wildest of living fowl. We and they had found a common home in the remote fastnesses of space and time; we were both back in the Pleistocene. Had we been able to, we would have bugled back their greeting. Now, from the far reaches of the years, I see them wheeling still.

—Aldo Leopold
from *A Sand County Almanac and Sketches Here and There*
copyright 1949
with permission of Oxford University Press, Inc.

The Heron

A HERON WENT WADING EARLY one morning to fish for his breakfast in a shallow stream. There were many fish in the water, but the stately heron thought he could find better. "Such small fry is certainly not suitable fare for a heron," he remarked to himself. And as a choice young perch swam by, the heron tipped his long bill in the air and snapped, "No, sir, I certainly wouldn't open my beak for that!" The sun grew higher and all the fish left the shallows for the cool, deep middle of the stream. When the heron could find no trace of a fish left in the stream, he was very grateful to finally break his fast on a mere snail.

—Charles Santore
from *Aesop's Fables*

HOW LOVELY IT WAS IN the old days ... how warm, how joyful
... Men and lions ... starfish and tiny creatures - these and every
form of life have ended ... The cry of the cranes is heard no more
in the meadows; the hum of the cockchafers is silent in the linden
groves...

> excerpt from the end of "The Seagull"
> from *The Time of the Cranes* by Norma Johnston

THE MALLARDS CALL WITH evening from the reeds
And float with dawn midway on the water;
They sleep with their mates, it is said,
With white wings overlapping and tails a-sweep
Lest the frost should fall upon them.

As the stream that flows never returns,
And as the wind that blows is never seen,
My wife of this world has left me,
Gone I know not whither!
So here, on the sleeves of these clothes
She used to have me wear,
I sleep now all alone!

Cranes call flying to the reedy shore;
How desolate I remain
As I sleep alone!

> —Tajihi
> Composed in grief at the death of Tajahi's wife.
> the Nara period 710-784 AD
> from *The Manyosku: One Thousand Poems*

The Race Between the Crane And the Hummingbird

T HIS STORY MATCHES THE smallest and largest birds against each other in a race to see who will marry a beautiful wood duck. The scientific name for the wood duck (*Aix sponsa*) literally means "bride" or "promised one." The wood duck does look as though it has been prepared for a wedding, being the most brightly colored of any waterfowl found in North America. As with most birds, however, it is the male which has the more beautiful plumage. Both the male and female have feathers forming a flowing crest over their heads and colorful iridescent wings. The display of their many colors is important in pair-formation during the nesting season. These are the only North American perching ducks. Unlike other waterfowl, they nest in tree cavities and forage for acorns and nuts on the forest floor. Although the species was on the verge of extinction earlier in this century, the placement of man-made nest boxes in suitable breeding areas has allowed it to recover.

Anyone would think that a race between a crane and a hummingbird would be won easily by the hummingbird, who can so often be seen darting quickly among flowers, collecting nectar. It is one of the most agile of all birds, and not only can hover, but can even fly backwards. As ungainly as a crane looks, however, it can actually fly faster than a hummingbird and can reach 60 mph with a good tailwind. Moreover, as the story suggests, hummingbirds are not generally found flying in the evening. Their metabolism is so high that their heartbeat and breathing actually slow down when they are resting at night. This allows them to conserve energy. How these small birds are able to migrate as far as Central America and back every year is a mystery!

If it is any consolation for the wood duck, her disappointment at the crane's victory should be tempered by the fact that male cranes assist in incubating their mates' eggs and rearing the young, while male hummingbirds take no part in domestic duties.

A hummingbird and a crane were both in love with a beautiful wood duck. She preferred the hummingbird, who was as handsome as the crane was awkward. But the crane was so persistent that in order to get rid of him she finally told him that he must challenge Hummingbird to a race, and she would marry the winner. Hummingbird was so swift, almost like a flash of lightning, and Crane so slow and heavy, that she felt sure the hummingbird would win. But she did not know that the crane could fly all night.

They agreed to start from the nest of the wood duck, which was in a hollow of a tree in the forest. They would fly from there to the ocean, which was many days travel from where they were, and then return to the starting point. The one that returned first would be the winner.

At the word "Start!" Hummingbird darted off like an arrow and was out of sight in a moment, leaving Crane to follow slowly behind. He flew all day, and when evening came, he stopped to roost for the night. By this time he was far ahead. But Crane flew steadily all night long, passing Hummingbird soon after midnight. He kept going until about dawn, when he rested by a small creek.

Hummingbird woke up in the morning and flew on again, thinking how easily he would win the race, until he reached the creek where Crane had been resting. There he saw Crane spearing small fish with his long bill and enjoying a leisurely breakfast. He then flew swiftly out of sight and again left Crane far behind.

Crane finished his breakfast and started on, and when evening came he kept on as he had before. This time it was hardly midnight when he passed Hummingbird, asleep on a small limb once more, and in the morning he had finished his breakfast before Hummingbird was in sight. The next day he gained a little more, and on the fourth day he was spearing fish for lunch when Hummingbird passed him. On the fifth and sixth days it was late in the afternoon before Hummingbird caught up, and on the morning of the seventh day, Crane was a whole night's travel ahead. He took his time at breakfast and preened his feathers, since he was nearing the finish line and wanted to look as elegant as he could. When Hummingbird arrived in the afternoon, he found he had lost the race. Wood Duck was very disappointed, but kept her promise to marry the winner.

—A Cherokee folktale

In Search of Solitude

I NEVER TIRE IN MY SEARCH OF SOLITUDE;
I wander aimlessly along out-of-the-way trails
Where I have never been before,
The more I change my direction, the wilder the
*   road becomes.*
Suddenly I come to the bank of a raging river;
The path breaks off, all trails vanish.
No one is there for me to ask directions:
Only a lone egret beside the tall grass, glistening white.

—Huang Ching-jen
from *Sunflower Splendor,*
Three Thousand Years of Chinese Poetry

The Cry of a Crane

THE CRANE CRIES IN THE NINE MARSHES,
Its voice carries into the wilds;
The fish plunges into the deep, or lies by the inlet;
Pleasant is that garden,
It is planted with the tan trees,
Under them are fallen leaves.

...The crane cries in the Nine Marshes,
Its voice carries up to heaven;
The fish lies by the inlet, or...plunges into the deep;
Pleasant is that garden,
It is planted with tan trees,
Under them are fallen leaves.

Oldest extant poem in the world about a crane.
Offers homage to the wild crane.
translated by Bernhard Kalgren
From *The Book of Odes*

ASCENDING IN THE CLOUDS WITH THE CRANE AS VEHICLE.

Riding on the wind up to the confines of heaven.

Trending the emptiness of the highest atmosphere.

"Ling-hsu-yin" (Song of Cool Emptiness)
a Chinese lute tune consisting of the above three parts
—Robert H. van Gulik
from *The Lore of the Chinese Lute*

The Crane

WITH A PURE NOTE HE WELCOMES THE EVENING MOON,
With sad thoughts he stands on cold bulrush.
Red head and cheeks like Hsi-shih's;
Frosty feathers and beard all white like the
  Four Venerable Old Men's.
Beneath jasper clouds, moving and stopping restlessly;
To him the spirit of the white egret is coarse.
All day long without the companionship of a flock,
By the side of the gully he laments his shadow's solitude.

> Alluding to Ssu-hao, the "Four Venerable Whitebeards,"
> four legendary old men known for their integrity.
> Offers homage to the wild crane.
> —Tu Mu
> from *Sunflower Splendor;*
> *Three Thousand Years of Chinese Poetry*

Flying Crane Pavilion

OVER SEVEN HUNDRED years ago when Marco Polo traveled to China, he described Hangzou with its beautiful West Lake as without doubt the finest and most splendid city in the world. The West Lake is surrounded by mountains on which there are numerous temples and pagodas. Across a section of the Lake there is a handsome causeway with carved stone balustrades and small pavilions. The causeway joins the tip of the peninsula to the mainland forming an inner lake with waters which are always calm. On this peninsula there is a high hill known as Lonely Hill because in early times it was far from the city.

Towards the end of the Tenth Century AD, a poet-painter who wished to retire from the world and devote himself to his art, built himself a hut on Lonely Hill were he lived and worked. His name was Lin He-Qing. His only companion besides a servant-cook was a crane which he had reared himself. It was very tame. When Lin was not painting or composing poetry he spent his time making a beautiful garden around his hut. He planted more than three hundred plum trees. The blossom in springtime was a sight to be seen. So happy was Lin with his crane and his plum trees that people said he had the plum trees for his wife and the crane for a son. If he was away from home when visitors came the servant would call the crane to stay with the guest until his master returned. When the master came back and was sitting drinking tea or wine with his visitor and reciting his latest poems, the crane would spread its great wings and fly around overhead to add to the entertainment.

When Lin eventually died he was buried on Lonely Hill and his tomb can be seen there today. The crane died too, it was said it died of sorrow, and all the plum trees withered. The crane lies buried in a tomb near its master's. A hundred years after Lin's death a temple and a pavilion were built near his tomb to commemorate him. The temple no longer exists but the pavilion has been restored and a fine terrace has been built where his hut stood and hundreds of plum trees have been planted. It is called the Flying Crane Pavilion or Fang He Ting.

—Dorothea Hayward Scott
from a 1956 guide book about
the West Lake at Hangchow

ON AN EVENING WHEN THE SPRING MISTS
Trail over the wide sea,
And sad is the voice of the cranes
I think of my far-off home.

Thinking of home,
Sleepless I sit,
The cranes call amid the shore reeds,
Lost in the mists of spring.

—Otomo Yakamochi
from *The Manyosku: One Thousand Poems*

Part Four

The Dance
of the Whooping Cranes

T HEY WERE IN A TERRITORY a little west of the prairie's rim where old Slewfoot had fed on fire-plant. Dry weather had sucked up much of the water and the marsh had broad areas that were now firm and dry. The ponds showed plainly. They had withdrawn from the saw-grass and only lily pads troubled the water's surface. The Blue Peter ran across them, bright with yellow legs and painted face. A slight breath of air rippled across the marsh and the water rippled under it. The lily pads tipped, an instant, their broad shining leaves to the glint of the sun.

"Jest enough of a riffle," Penny said, "and the moon jest right."

He fastened lengths of line to the two poles and attached the deer-hair bobs.

"Now you work your bob acrost the north end and I'll try the south. Don't make no fuss, walkin.'"

Jody stood a moment to watch his father make an expert cast across the pond. He marveled at the skill of the knotted hands. The bob lay at the edge of a cluster of lily pads. Penny began to jerk it slowly across the water. It dipped and bobbed with the ir-regular rhythm of a live insect. There was no strike and Penny drew in his line and cast again in the same place. He called to an invisible fish, lurking near the weedy bottom.

"Now Grandpappy, I kin see you sittin' there on your stoop." He jerked the bob more slowly. " You better lay down your pipe and come git your dinner."

Jody tore himself from the fascination of his father's perform-ance and moved to his end of the pond. He cast badly for a time, tingling his line and laying his bob in the most unlikely places; over-reaching the narrow pond and enmeshing the hook in the tough saw-grass. Then something of harmony came to him. He felt his arm swing in a satisfying arc. His wrist flexed at the proper moment. He laid the bob exactly where he had meant to, at the edge of a patch of switch-grass.

Penny called, "Mighty nice, son. Leave it lay jest a minute. Then git ready the first second you jerk it."

He had not known his father was watching. He was tense. He jerked his pole cautiously and the bob flipped across the water. There was a swirl, a silver form shot half clear of the water, an open mouth as big as a cook-pot enveloped the bob. A weight like a millstone dropped at the end of his line, fought like a wild-cat, and pulled him off-balance. He braced himself against the frenzy to which he was irrevocably attached.

Penny called, "Take it easy. Don't let him git under them bon-nets. Keep the tip o' your pole up. Don't give him no slack."

Penny left him to the struggle. His arms ached from the strain. He was afraid to tug too hard for fear of breaking the line. He dared not yield an inch for fear a sudden slackness would tell the loss of the giant. He longed for magic words from his father, indi-cating some miracle by which he might land his fish and be done with the torment. The bass was sulking. It made a dash for the grasses, where it might tangle the line around their stems and so rip free. It came to Jody that if he walked around the edges of pond, keeping a taut line, he might lead the bass into shallow water and flounder him at the edge. He worked cautiously. He was tempted to drop the pole and clutch the line itself and come to grips with his adversary. He began to walk away from the pond. He gave his pole a heave and landed the bass, flouncing, in the grass. He dropped the pole and ran, to move the catch to a final safety. The bass would weigh ten pounds. Penny came to him.

"Boy, I'm proud of you. Nobody couldn't have handled him better."

Jody stood panting. Penny thumped him on the back, as excited as he. He looked down, unbelieving, at the stout form and the great maw.

"I feel as good as if 'twas ol' Slewfoot," he said, and they grinned together and pummeled each other's backs.

"Now I got to go beat you," Penny said.

They took separate ponds. Penny called that he was licked and beaten. He began fishing for Ma Baxter's bream with a hand-line and bonnet worms. Jody cast and cast again, but there was never the mad swirl of waters, the great leap, the live and struggling weight. He caught a small bass and held it up to show his father.

"Throw him back," Penny called. "We don't need him for eatin.' Leave him to grow up big as t'other one. Then we'll come back again and ketch him."

Jody put the small fish back reluctantly and watched it swim away. His father was stern about not taking more of anything, fish or game, then could be eaten or kept. Hope of another monster dwindled as the sun finished its spring arc of the daylight sky. He cast leisurely, taking his pleasure in his increasingly dexterity of arm and wrist. The moon was now wrong. It was no longer feed-time. The fish were not striking. Suddenly he heard his father whistle like a quail. It was the signal they used together in squirrel hunting. Jody laid down his pole and looked back to make sure he could identify the tuft of grass where he had covered his bass from the rays of the sun. He walked cautiously to where his father beckoned.

Penny whispered, "Foller me. We'll ease up clost as we dare."

He pointed, "The whoopin' cranes is dancin.'"

Jody saw the great white birds in the distance. His father's eye, he thought, was like an eagle's. They crouched on all fours and crept forward slowly. Now and then Penny dropped flat on his stomach and Jody dropped behind him. They reached a clump of high saw-grass and Penny motioned for concealment behind it. The birds were so close that it seemed to Jody he might touch them with his long fishing pole. Penny squatted on his haunches and Jody followed. His eyes were wide. He made a count of the whooping cranes. There were sixteen.

The cranes were dancing a cotillion as surely as it was danced at Volusia. Two stood apart, erect and white, making a strange music that was part cry and part singing. The rhythm was irregular, like the dance. The other birds were in a circle. In the heart of the circle, several moved counter-clock-wise. The musicians made their music. The dancers raised their wings and lifted their feet, first one and then the other. They sank their heads deep in their snowy breasts, lifted them and sank them again. They moved soundlessly, part awkwardness, part grace. The dance was solemn, wings fluttered, raising and falling like out-stretched arms. The outer circle shuffled around and around. The group in the center attained a slow frenzy.

Suddenly all motion ceased. Jody thought the dance was over, or that the intruders had been discovered. Then the two musicians joined the circle. Two others took their places. There was a pause. The dance was resumed. The birds were reflected in the clear marsh water. Sixteen white shadows reflected the motions. The evening breeze moved across the saw-grass. It bowed and fluttered. The water rippled. The setting sun lay rosy on the white bodies. Magic birds were dancing in a mystic marsh. The grass swayed with them, and the shallow waters, and the earth fluttered under them. The earth was dancing with the cranes, and the low sun, and the wind and sky.

Jody found his own arms lifting and falling with his breath, as the cranes' wings lifted. The sun was sinking into the saw-grass. The marsh was golden. The whooping cranes were washed with gold. The far hammocks were black. Darkness came to the lily pads, and the water blackened. The cranes were whiter than any clouds, or any white bloom of oleander or of lily. Without warning, they took flight. Whether the hour-long dance was, simply, done, or whether the long nose of an alligator had lifted above the water to alarm them, Jody could not tell, but they were gone. They made a great circle against the sunset, whooping their strange rusty cry that sounded only in their flight. They flew in a long line into the west, and vanished.

Penny and Jody straightened and stood up. They were cramped from the long crouching. Dusk lay over the saw-grass, so that the ponds were scarcely visible. The world was shadow, melting into shadow. They turned to the north. Jody found his bass. They cut to the east, to leave the marsh behind them, then north again. The trail was dim in the growing darkness. It joined the scrub road and they turned once more east, continuing now in a certainty, for the dense growth of the shrub boarded the road like walls. The shrub was black and the road was a dark gray strip of carpet, sandy and soundless. Small creatures darted across in front of them and scurried in the bushes. In the distance, a panther screamed. Bull-bats shot low over their heads. They walked in silence.

At the house, bread was baked and waiting, and hot fat was in the iron skillet. Penny lighted a fat-wood torch and went to the lot to do his chores. Jody scaled and dressed the fish at the back stoop, where a ray of light glimmered from the fire on the hearth.

Ma Baxter dipped the pieces in meal and fried them crisp and golden. The family ate without speaking.

She said, "What ails you fellers?"

They did not answer. They had no thoughts for what they ate nor for the woman. They were no more than conscious that she spoke to them. They had seen a thing that was unearthly. They were in a trance from the spell of its beauty.

—Marjorie Kinnan Rawlings
from *The Yearling*
reprinted with the permission of Simon & Schuster

The Advengers of Ibycus

THE LYRIC POET, IBYCUS, WAS walking alone on the country road when a band of robbers set upon him mortally wounding him. As he lay dying a flight of cranes passed overhead, so he called out to them, "Bear witness to this deed!" No one could discover how Ibycus met his death.

Later that year the same band of robbers was mingling with the crowd in the Corinth market place. When a flight of cranes passed overhead, one of the robbers said to the other without thinking, "There go the advengers of the death of Ibycus!" He was overheard and the group was summoned for questioning, Eventually they admitted their guilt and paid the price for their wicked deed.

When robbers once to deserts came,
O Ibycus thy blood to spill:
Thou didst beseech a cloud of cranes
To witness their accursed will.
And not in vain; the Furies brought
Revenge on them in Corinth land...

Ever afterwards if a mystery was solved by some strange means, people would remark, "Ah, the cranes of Ibycus!"

—Edward Topsell
from *The Fowles of Heaven* or *History of Birdes*

Platte River Sunset

WE ARE OUT LOOKING *for signs of the early spring*
which has come to the midlands.
Driving over a rutted road
we curve around the corner
and bump westward toward the late day sun.
Down a space, beyond the corner,
a farm lane angles through a vacant gate,
end-stopped by rough barked tree posts
leaning to the pull of the rusting barbed wire.

A large and shallow pond along the east fence line
is neatly covered by a paddling of mallards,
food searching on the muddy bottom,
popping curly tail feathers skyward,
righting themselves, regaining dignity,
and carrying on soft
contralto conversations with each other.

In the pasture west of the ducks,
the winter-grayed brome grass is a tufty carpet
for hundreds of slim-stemmed sandhill cranes
whose dove soft color is head crowned
by a white tonsure edged in scarlet.
An occasional pair, here and there,
performs a courtship galliard,
leaping high, settling back;
others' necks dart suddenly downward, ess up
with a morsel of the first spring greens.

Suddenly, the ducks take noisy quacking flight;
a few cranes stretch upward, lift,
are flying, circling, spiraling higher.
More join in, and more and more and more,
and the sky is filling with cranes
and the rush of wings
and their flying call

like hundreds of wooden wind chimes
fluting above the earth.

The sun, hanging orange just over the hill,
lights them upward and off
to a river island roost.
And they are gone.
And the sound of the wings and flutes
are gone.
And we wheel bound waters,
who can leave only by the rutted road,
finally breathe again.

—Carol Miles Petersen
first published in the *Kansas Quarterly* under "Untitled"

Why Crane's Feathers Are Brown And Otter Doesn't Feel the Cold

THERE WAS ONCE A season when Crane laid her egg after all the other birds were already hatching their young. Crane laid the egg so late that the young Crane did not have time to learn to fly before summer was done.

Crane spoke to Otter. "My son is too young to fly South with us. Keep him with you until I return in the Spring."

"I will do it," Otter said, and he took the young Crane to live in his den.

One day Otter went hunting. The young Crane was alone. Then Osni, that is, Cold, came into the den and took the young Crane away.

"You stay with me," Osni said. "You will do what I tell you to do," he said, and he took the young Crane to his lodge.

Every day the young Crane did what Osni commanded him. And all day and all night young Crane tended the fire and kept it going. He stirred the hot ashes with his bill so that it was blackened by the fire. He fanned the hot coals with his wings so that the feathers were singed brown by the heat.

Spring came. The young Crane went out of the lodge when Osni was not looking.

"Mother," the young Crane called. "Mother come and find me."

Otter heard the young Crane. Otter went up the mountain. He went to the cave of Thunder and Lightning. "Help me," Otter said. "Help me get the young Crane away from Osni."

"We will do it," they said.

"We have come for the young Crane," Otter said to Osni.

"He is my grandson," Osni said. "I want him with me."

"He is not your grandson," Otter said. "Give him up."

"No," Osni said.

"Do it," Thunder said.

"Let the young Crane go with Otter," Lightning said.

"No," Osni said.

"Well, then," Thunder said.

"We shall see," Lightning said.

Thunder struck Osni with his wings. Lightning tore Osni with his claws. Osni, that is, Cold, fell down in front of his lodge.

Crane came. "You have saved my son," she said. "I will give you a feast," she said to Thunder and Lightning. "I will give you a feast," she said to Otter, "and I will make you a gift. You will not feel cold in the winter. You will swim, you will run, you will hunt when the cold is great and the snow is deep, but you will not feel the cold because you took care of my son for me."

—Natalia M. Belting
from *The Long-tailed Bear and Other Indian Legends*
A tale told by the Assiniboin Indians, a branch of
the Dakota, living in the valleys of the
Saskatchewan and Assiniboin rivers in Canada.

The Crane Maiden Story

O NCE UPON A TIME THERE was a man called Tien Kun-lun. He was very poor, and was not able to marry a wife. In the land he owned there was a pond which was deep, clear and beautiful. Once when the crops were ripe he went to his field and saw that there were three beautiful girls washing themselves and bathing in the pond. Wanting to have a closer look at them he watched them from a hundred paces away. Two of them at once changed into white cranes, and flew away, but the third stayed in the pond, washing herself.

Tien Kun-lun pressed low down between the cornstalks and crept forward to look at her. These beautiful girls were heavenly maidens. The older ones clasped their heavenly robes and rode off into the sky, but the youngest, who was in the pond, did not dare come out. She made no secret of this, saying to Kun-lun: "We three sisters, who are Heavenly Maidens, came out to amuse ourselves for awhile in this pond. But you, the owner of the pond, saw us. My two elder sisters were able to rescue their heavenly robes in time and escape. But I, the youngest, lingered all alone in the pond, and you have taken away my heavenly robe and I cannot come naked out of the pond. Please do me the kindness to give it back to me, that I may cover my nakedness and come out of the pond. If you do so, I will marry you." But Kun-lun debated the matter in his mind and decided that if he gave her the heavenly robe, there was a danger that she might fly away. So he answered: "Madam, it is no use your asking for your heavenly robe, for you will never get it. But how would it be if I were to take off my shirt, so that for the time being you could cover yourself with that?"

At first the Heavenly Maiden refused to come out on these terms, and Kun-lun at last declared that it was getting dark and he must go. She tried to detain him, still asking for her robe, but when she found she could not get it, her tone changed and she said to Kun-lun, "Very well then! Give me your shirt to cover me while I come out of the pond, and I will marry you." Kun-lun was delighted. He rolled up the heavenly robe and hid it away. Then he took off his shirt and gave it to the Heavenly Maiden, to cover her when she came out of the pond. She said to Kun-lun, "Do not be afraid I shall go away. Let me put on my heavenly robe again, and I will go along with you." But Kun-lun would rather have died than give it to her, and without more ado he took her home with him to show her to his mother. The mother was delighted and ordered mats to be set out. All the friends and

144

relatives of the family were invited and on the appointed day the girl was hailed as New Bride. Although she was a Heavenly Maiden, they lived together as man and wife. Days went and months came, and presently she bore him a son, a fine child, whom they named Tien Qang.

Soon afterwards Kun-lun was marked down for service in the west, and was away a long time. The Heavenly Maid said to herself, "It is three years since my husband went away and I have been bringing up this child." Then she said to her mother-in-law, "I am a Heavenly Maiden. At the time I came, when I was small and young, my father made for me a heavenly robe, and with it I rode through the sky and came here. If I were to see that robe now, I wonder what size it would be. Let me have a look at it; I would dearly love to see it!"

Now on the day that Kun-lun went away, he had given strict orders to his mother, saying, "This is Heavenly Maiden's robe. Keep it hidden away and do not let her see it. For if she sees it, she will certainly ride away with it through the sky, and will never be seen again." So they hid it away, and Kun-lun went off to the west.

After he when away, the Heavenly Maiden thought constantly about the robe, fretting about it all the time and never knowing a moment's happiness. She said to her mother-in-law, "Do let me just have a look at the heavenly robe!" She kept on worrying her about this, and at last her mother-in-law decided to fall in with her wish. So she told her daughter-in-law to go outside the gate for a little while and then quietly come back. She went out at once and the mother-in-law took out the heavenly robe from its hiding place and when the Heavenly Maiden came back, showed it to her. When she saw it, her heart was cut to the quick, her tears fell like floods of rain, and she longed to ride off through the air. But having thought out no plan to do this, she had to give the robe back to her mother-in-law, who again hid it away.

Less than ten days later she said once more to her mother-in-law, "Let me have another look at my heavenly robe." The mother-in-law said, "I was afraid you might put it on, and fly away from us." The daughter-in-law said, "I was once a Heavenly

Maiden. But now I am married to your son and we have a child. How can you think I would leave you? Such a thing is impossible." The mother-in-law gave in, but was still afraid that she might fly away, and set someone to keep strict watch at the main gate.

But the Heavenly Maiden, as soon as she had put on the robe, flew straight up into the sky through the roof vent. The old woman beat her breast and in great distress hurried out of the door to see what happened to her. She arrived in time to see her soaring away into the sky. The mother-in-law, when she knew that she had lost her daughter-in-law, let out such a cry as pierced the bright sky; her tears fell like rain, she became utterly desperate and in the bitter sorrow of her heart all day she would not eat.

The Heavenly Maiden had passed more than five years in the world of men, and now she had spent her first two days in heaven above. When she escaped and reached her home both her sisters cursed her for shameless baggage. "By marrying that common creature of a world of men," they said, "you have made your father and mother so sad they do nothing but weep." "However," they said, "it is no good your continually lamenting for your son as you are doing now. Tomorrow we three sisters will go together and play at the pool. Then you will certainly see your child again."

The child Tien Qang had just reached his fifth year. At that time there was a certain Master Tung Zhung who was always seeking for persons of superior conduct. He knew that this was the child of a Heavenly Maiden and knew that the Heavenly Maiden was about to come down to the lower world. So he said to the child, "Just at midday go to the side of the pond and look. Three women will come all dressed in white silk robes. Two of them will raise their heads and look at you; but one will lower her head and pretend not to see you, and that one will be your mother."

Tien Qang did as Tung Zhung told him, and just at midday he saw beside the pond three Heavenly Maidens, all dressed in white silk robes, cutting salad-herbs at the edge of the pond. Tien Qang went nearer and looked at them. Seeing him from afar they knew that it was the child who had come, and the two elders sisters said to the younger, "Your child has come." Then he called out to his mother. But she, although she hung her head in shame and did not look at him, could not stop her sorrow from coming out of her heart, and she wept bitterly. The three sisters then took their heavenly robes and carried the child away with them into the sky.

Tun-huang in the far north-west of China is the site of the Caves of the Thousand Buddhas carved into the living rock. In 1900 a Taoist monk, while restoring one of the many Fresco paintings on the stone walls of the caves found that the underneath surface was brick not stone. Carefully removing one brick he peered in and discovered a smaller cave piled high with rolls of manuscripts. The cave had been bricked up some nine hundred years earlier to protect the monastery library from invaders. The manuscripts date from the fourth to the tenth centuries AD. Most are Buddhist texts but some eighty pieces of popular literature were found and among them *The Crane Maiden* story.

—Arthur Waley
abbreviated from *Ballads and Stories from Tun-huang: An Anthology*

Remembering the Crane I Released

LIVING IN RETIREMENT AT WU-HSI
A villager gave me a fledgling crane.
A year later, its feathers grown,
Pitying its yearning to fly,
I released it from its cage.
It soared into the sky
Circling round and round
Before finally leaving me.

Its feathers white as unsullied snow
It gazed at its own reflection
And danced with the white clouds
Mirrored in the Autumn pond
Like a celestrial being from the fairy isles.
The lingering echo of its ringing cry resounded in the skies.

It soared with the wind and seemed to brush past the sun.
"Do not regret leaving me! Your destiny is to reach heaven!"
I sat and watched it disappeared into the blue
Pitying the herons and the loons which must grow old by the
river bank.

—Li Shen
from *The Complete Poems of the Tang Dynasty*
Concerns relationship between crane and man.

The Trap

A GIANT CLAM CAME UP ON the sandy shore to enjoy the noonday sun. From the sky, a crane spied the clam and flew down to enjoy a hearty meal. As soon as the crane inserted his beak in the shell's slit, the clam clapped his shell shut on the crane's beak, locking the latter with an iron grip.

Presently the clam said, "If you are not able to fly away in a day or two, you will die of starvation."

To which the crane replied, "If it doesn't rain within a day or two, you will die of thirst."

While they were arguing, a fisherman came by and took the two prisoners away.

Moral: In the face of mutual destruction, it is fatal to waste time in a debate.

—Isabelle C. Chang
from *Tales from Old China*

A Pair of Cranes Bathing in a Brook

LATE IN SPRING I VISITED A friend in Kuan-k'ou. A pair of cranes were dancing in a clear rivulet. I observed their feathers white as snow, and the top of their heads red like vermilion. They fluttered up and down, and took their bath while dancing. Then they spread their wings and flew high up in the sky, and cried in harmony in the azure vault, making me doubt whether they were not Immortals.

Introduction from
"T'ien-wen-ko-ch'in-pu-chi-ch'eng"
A Chinese lute tune
—Robert H. van Gulik
from *The Lore of the Chinese Lute*

The Cranes at
Minden Bridge:
All and Spring

WE CATCH NATURE BEST IN FLIGHT,
But, ah, sparks among the stubble, red cropped cranes at rest
Where lamps are lit against the night!

Yet, flocks framed now by flaming sun, the sight
Against the water in that sunlight dressed –
We catch nature best in flight.

Sound of those ten thousand times ten thousands' might
Rises off the fields whose soil is stardust God expressed
Where lamps are lit against the night.

From north and south they rise, take a measure of air's height,
Converge the water's coursing east to west.
We catch nature best in flight.

It seems in their descent that all lost tribes unite,
Release us, watching, from our dark dividedness, arrest
Where lamps are lit against the night.

Bereft such splendor, nature's fragile web in us is slight,
Yet we among its company are confessed
Where lamps are lit against the night.
We catch nature best in flight.

—Charles A. Peek
April 2, 1999

Sandhill Cranes Visit This Area on Their Way North

(First known article to be published about
the Nebraska crane migration)

B ETWEEN GRAND ISLAND and Kearney the Platte River di-
vides into several channels. In the spring the grasslands between and along these channels become marsh-like with melting
snow and rain. This environment attracts great flocks of cranes,
known as the Sandhill Crane, or Grus Mexicana.

Eleven years ago we moved to the south side of the Platte
River, I shall never forget the amazement I felt the first time these
spectacular birds floated into our valley and landed on the grasslands near the river. At first we were attracted by the strange rolling call, similar to the amplified purr of a cat, with much emphasis on the trilling of the 'r'r'r'! Looking skyward we beheld long
irregular lines of enormous birds, necks outstretched and long legs
trailing, flying to the river. They continued coming from the
southeast until several thousand clustered along the river banks.
As night fell their chatter quieted. We were puzzled, wondering
what migration we had just witnessed.

In the years that followed we learned many things about the
behavior pattern of the Sandhill Crane. Late in February or early
March, depending on the break in the winter, the cranes appear
and seem to enjoy congregating as if having a spring convention.
They leave us on a warm day in April. Hundreds sweep into the
sky and wheel about until all join in one flock and become a
compact circling mass. Using field glasses we have watched this
cloud of birds mount higher and higher until they vanish. The
valley seems deserted and lonely for a few days after their departure.

During the summer the cranes disperse in the Pacific North-
west where they breed and raise their young. The nests are loosely
constructed of grass, near a stream or lake. Their two eggs are
olive green and spotted with burnt umber. Young cranes emerge

from their shells covered with down and capable of running about at once.

The fall flight southward is seldom seen. Two years we saw them, once in September and again in October. There was an urgency in their manner and they passed over us flying very high. Winter finds them around the Gulf of Mexico. We have identified small flocks over the Everglades in Florida and near Corpus Christi, Texas.

Turning to the book "Birds of America," John James Audubon gives the following description: Height four feet, wing spread seven and one-half feet, plumage slate gray, long neck with a rather small head and long black bill, red patch near the eye, long black legs. Standing on the ground this bird may easily observe the approach of danger. The sturdy bill is used to unearth roots, bulbs, and tender green shoots. If pressed to defend himself this bill serves well as a dagger. Normally a peaceful bird, the crane will fight courageously if forced into adverse circumstances. The food most desired is grain, especially corn, insects, frogs, snakes and mice.

Isolation and privacy are highly desired, so if disturbed too often they move up or down the river where they may feel more secure.

In Nebraska the cranes are protected from hunters by a fine of $100 per bird. Our pioneers roasted the birds and enjoyed the mild dark meat, comparing it to turkey in texture and flavor.

It is amusing to see the birds leap and flap their wings in an effort to become airborne. This awkwardness disappears as soon as the powerful wings raise them up. Wheeling and sliding overhead they portray only grace and beauty. At sunrise they fly upland to the corn fields to feed. Late in the afternoon the flight returns to the sloughs along the river. Imagine the drama of a flaming sunset, the valley tinged with spring's first green, a blue mist veiling the river, and hundred of cranes gliding above on motionless wings.

The odd dance the cranes perform is most spectacular. In a grassy meadow where water forms brooks and ponds, the birds will gather to splash and preen their feathers. Suddenly two birds begin bowing to each other and leaping into the air in unison. Others join in the dance, by couples, until the scene becomes a seething mass of lithe jumpers, chattering gleefully throughout the performance. This is not the courtship dance, as many think, for they may execute this feat any time during the year. I think it is an outlet for high spirits and an expression of joyous living.

The cranes can usually be seen during this month on the river road west of Doniphan.

—Lillian R. Amick
Printed around 1948 by
The Grand Island Independent newspaper

THE CRANE CRIES IN THE mashes, its sound is heard in the skies.

—Robert H. van Gulik
from *The Lore of the Chinese Lute*
cry of the crane said to penetrate unto Heaven

Overlooking the Desert

CLEAR AUTUMN. I GAZE OUT INTO
Endless spaces. The horizon
Wavers in bands of haze. Far off
The river flows into the sky.
The lone city is blurred with smoke.
The wind blows the last leaves away.
The hills grow dim as the sun sets.
A single crane flies late to roost.
The twilit trees are full of crows.

—Tu Fu

A Second Home

There is in our small town –
Nestled in San Luis
Valley – a family
With two boys and two girls

All deaf. Two times each year –
For Christmas and summer
Vacation – they come home
From the School for the Deaf

Which is also their home.
Long before these children,
Before prairie schooners,
Before indigenous

Peoples, there were cranes, some
Whooping, but most Sandhill,
Great gray birds, some five feet
Tall, wings spread eight feet long

During their graceful flight.
Like the deaf children, they
Migrate twice each year to
This valley, a second

Home. Like the deaf children,
Their voices are strange to
Us, muted gongs from a
Distant monastery.

—Art Washburn

The Crane Wife

ONCE THERE WAS A MAN named Karoku. He lived with his seventy-year-old mother far back in the mountains, where he made charcoal for a living. One winter, as he was going to the village to buy some futon (bedding), he saw a crane struggling in a trap where it had been caught. Just as Karoku was stopping to release the poor crane, the man who had set the trap came running up.

"What are you doing, interfering with other people's business?" he cried.

"I felt so sorry for the crane I thought I would let it go. Will you sell it to me? Here, I have the money I was going to use to buy futon. Please take the money, and let me have the crane."

The man agreed, and Karoku took the crane and immediately let it fly away free.

"We may get cold tonight," thought Karoku, returning home, "but it can't be helped." When he got home, his mother asked what he had done with the futon. He replied, "I saw a crane caught in a trap. I felt so sorry for it that I used all the money to buy it and set it free."

"Well," his mother said, "since you have done it, I suppose that it is all right."

The next evening, just as night was falling, a beautiful young woman such as he had never seen before came to Karoku's house. "Please let me spend the night here," she asked, but Karoku refused, saying, "My little hut is too poor." She replied, "No, I do not mind; please, I implore you, let me stay," until finally he consented, and she was allowed to spend the night. During the evening she said, "I have something I should like to discuss with you," and when Karoku asked what it was, she replied, "I beg of you, please make me your wife."

Karoku, greatly surprised, said: "This is the first time in my life that I have seen such a beautiful woman as you. I am a very poor man; I do not even know where my next meal is coming from; how could I ever take you as my wife?"

"Please do not refuse," she pleaded; "please take me as your wife."

"Well, as you beg me so much, I don't know what to do," he replied. When his mother heard of this, she said to the woman, "Since you insist, you may become my son's bride. Please stay here and work hard." Soon preparations were made, and they were married.

Some time after this Karoku's wife said, "Please let me go into the weaving room and leave me there for three days. Close the door tightly and be sure not to open it to look at me." Her husband shut her into the weaving room, and on the fourth day, she came out. "It must have been very unpleasant in there," he said. "I was worried about you. Hurry and have something to eat."

After she finished eating she said, "Karoku, please take this cloth that I have woven and sell it for two thousand ryo." So saying, she gave the piece of cloth to her husband. He took it to the lord of the province, who, when he saw it, said, "This is very beautiful material, I will pay you two or even three thousand ryo for it. Can you bring me another piece like it?"

"I must ask my wife if she can weave another, " Karoku replied.

"Oh, you need not ask her; it is all right if only you agree. I will give you the money for it now," the lord said.

Karoku returned home and told his wife what the lord had said.

"Just give me time and I'll weave another piece," she said. "This time please shut me in the room for one week. During that time you must be sure not to open the door and look at me."

By the time the week was nearly over, Karoku became very worried about his wife. On the last day of the week, he opened the door to see if she was all right. There inside the room was a crane, naked after having pulled out all her beautiful long feathers. She was using her feathers to weave the cloth and was just at the point of finishing it. The crane cried out, "I have finished the cloth, but since you have seen who I really am, I am afraid that you can no longer love me. I must return to my home. I am not a person but the crane whom you rescued. Please take the cloth to the lord as you promised." After she had said this, the crane silently turned toward the west. When she did this, thousands of cranes appeared and, taking her with them, they all flew out of sight.

Karoku had become a rich man, but he wanted to see his beloved wife so badly that he could not bear it. He searched for her throughout Japan until he was exhausted. One day as he was sitting on the seashore resting, he saw an old man alone in a rowing boat, approaching from the open ocean. "How strange," thought Karoku. "Where could he be coming from; there are no islands near here." As he sat in bewilderment, the boat landed on the beach. Karoku called out, "Grandfather, where did you come from?"

"I came from an island called 'The Robe of Crane Feathers.'" the old man replied.

"Would you please take me to that island?" asked Karoku.

The man quickly agreed, and Karoku climbed into the boat. The boat sped over the water, and in no time they had arrived at a beautiful white beach. They landed, and when Karoku got out of the boat and turned around, the boat and the old man had vanished from sight.

Karoku walked up the beach and soon came to a beautiful lake. In the middle of the lake was an island, and there on the island was the naked crane. She was surrounded by a myriad of cranes, for she was queen of the cranes. Karoku stayed a short while and was given a feast. Afterwards the old man with the boat returned, and Karoku was taken back to his home.

translated by Robert J. Adams
from *Folk Tales of Japan*
Collected from oral tradition by scholarly Japanese folklorists.
The story has been made into a popular drama.

Part Five

The Gratitude of the Crane

Another variation of the story about a
wounded crane's gratitude towards its rescuers.

T HE ISLANDS OF JAPAN EXTEND like a string of pearls in the
azure sea. On the northernmost pearl—the island of Hok-
kaido—there once lived an old woodcutter and his wife.

Life was not easy for the old couple. Each day the man had to
travel a little further from home to find enough firewood to sell,
and each day his legs and back grew a little stiffer with age. Some
days the woodcutter returned with only enough sticks to light the
tiny stove in their home. Some days he returned with none at all.

On one such day during the grip of winter, the woodcutter was
heading home empty-handed when he was startled to find a crane
lying across his path. On closer inspection, the woodcutter saw
that one of the bird's wings had been pierced by an arrow. Another man might have rejoiced at the discovery of such a promis-
ing meal, but the woodcutter's only thought was for the crane's
comfort.

"Here now," said the woodcutter soothingly. "Just hold still,
and I'll have that arrow out in no time." Slowly and carefully, all

the while calming the bird with his talk, the woodcutter eased the arrow from the crane's wing. He wiped away the blood and cleaned the wound with a bit of water from his canteen. The bird rose to its feet, arched its graceful neck, and hesitantly flexed first one wing and then the other. Then, with a running start, the majestic creature leapt into the air and flew away.

During dinner that evening, the woodcutter told his wife about the wounded crane. "You did well to help the poor creature, " she told him. "The crane is no ordinary bird. It should not be treated otherwise."

Just as the two were finishing their meal, there was a knock at the door. The woodcutter rose to answer it. A small girl, who appeared to be no more than ten years of age, stood there. Her clothes were tattered and torn, and much too thin to ward off the chill of the winter's night.

"Kind sir," the girl said, bowing deeply, "I have lost my way, and the night is cold. May I warm myself by your fire?"

The old man hurried the girl inside, seating her by the stove into which he threw some more sticks. His wife brought her a steaming bowl of miso soup. Clutching it for some time between her hands to warm them, the girl greedily drank it down.

"Child, why are you alone in the woods on such a night as this?" asked the old woman. "Where are your parents? Where is your home?"

"I have no parents," replied the girl. "At least none that I can remember. I was hoping to make it as far as the next village when I lost my way in the dark."

Never having been blessed with children, the woodcutter and his wife looked at one another and had the very same thought. "Then you must stay with us,' they said. The girl thanked them and agreed to share their home.

Megumi (may-Goo-mee), as the young girl was called, had been favored with a disposition as sweet as plum wine. Each morning she awoke with a smile. She sang as she helped cook and clean the house; she skipped and pranced when she accompanied the woodcutter on his rounds. She was just as popular with the children her own age. She was eagerly sought out as a playmate by the boys and girls in the village, who laughed in delight when she danced for them, leaping into the air, her arms aflutter.

"Megumi has brought us such happiness," the woodcutter said to his wife one evening.

"Indeed she has, husband!" exclaimed the old woman. "I think often of the crane you saved in the woods that day. The gods must have seen fit to repay you in this way."

While the woodcutter and his wife never spoke of it, Megumi knew life was a constant struggle for them. One morning she said, "I know how hard it is to stock the larder and keep the house warm. Please allow me to help you. I am a skilled weaver. If I had a loom, I could weave a bolt of cloth that you could then sell."

The old man and his wife were reluctant to put the young girl to work in this way, but Megumi insisted and so the woodcutter built a loom for her. When it was done, the girl told the couple, "It will take seven days for me to weave the cloth. During that time, I must not be disturbed. Please do not worry about me, but please do not take even one peek at me while I am at my work." The old man and woman promised to honor Megumi's wishes.

Seven days later, when Megumi emerged from her room, the woodcutter and his wife were alarmed by the girl's appearance. Her face had no color and she was painfully thin. But their attention turned to the bolt of shimmering cloth that the girl held in her arms. It was unlike anything they had ever seen. The intricately woven pattern seemed to dance with life, yet the cloth was as light as a feather. It was most exquisite.

Megumi smiled and said, "This cloth should fetch a good price at the market. But do not set the price yourself. Let those who desire it offer what they think it is worth."

On market day, the woodcutter took the bolt of cloth to the village. He had hardly unwrapped it when a clothier stopped to stare at it, overwhelmed by the dazzling design.

"I'll give you one hundred gold pieces for this," the clothier said without hesitation. The woodcutter remembered what Megumi had said about letting others set the cloth's price. He was amazed to think that someone was offering one hundred gold pieces for it. His thoughts were interrupted by another bystander shouting, "I'll give you five hundred!"

"I'll double that!" declared a third. "This fabric is fit for the gods! I am the Emperor's tailor, and this cloth will make a splendid robe for His Royal Highness. Take my offer of one thousand gold pieces."

A murmur of excitement ran through the crowd of people that had gathered around the woodcutter. One thousand gold pieces! An unheard of price for a bolt of cloth. But the Emperor's tailor was already counting out the coins, and so the woodcutter gave him the cloth in exchange for a bulging sack of gold.

Megumi only smiled knowingly when the woodcutter showed his wife the coins. "First you and now this," the two old people said, hugging the girl. "How can we ever thank you for the happiness you've brought us?"

"Dear ones, you have done much more than that for me," Megumi replied simply.

The three lived well for many years until there were only a few coins left in the money jar. "It is time I wove you some more fabric," announced Megumi one morning. "Please remember what I once told you. You must not disturb me while I am at my work, and you must not, under any circumstances, even glance at me while I am weaving." Once again, the old man and his wife agreed to Megumi's conditions.

Perhaps if the neighbors hadn't raised such doubts in their minds, the old couple would have found it easy to do as Megumi bid. But first one busybody and then another questioned why the old man and his wife should not watch the fabulous fabric taking shape. "Our daughters keep no secrets from us," they scoffed. "Besides, she's just weaving a piece of cloth. What harm can there be in watching her do it?"

"Megumi has asked us not to watch her, and we must abide by her wishes," the old woman explained. However, she had to admit that she did wonder what went on behind that closed door. She recalled how thin and pale Megumi had been after she'd woven the first bolt of cloth. And just how did the girl weave cloth without using thread of any sort?

For six of the seven days, the old woman resisted the urge to spy on Megumi. But on the afternoon of the seventh day, she could hold back no longer. "Surely just a quick peek will do no harm," she thought to herself. "Megumi must be nearly done by now anyway." The old woman approached the door on tiptoe, and carefully opened it just a crack.

What she saw was truly shocking. There at the loom stood a blood-spattered crane, frantically pulling feathers from its own body and weaving them into cloth. The old woman suppressed a cry, then fainted and slumped to the ground.

When she came to, she saw that both her husband and Megumi were kneeling beside her. The girl held one of the woman's hands in her own, and reached for one of the woodcutter's before lowering her eyes. "I am so sorry that it had to end like this," she said, her voice barely above a whisper. "As you have already guessed, I am the crane whose life you saved so many years ago."

"I was allowed to become a human child, the one thing you had never had, so that I might repay the kindness you showed me. There was only one condition: If ever you were to discover my true identity, I would have to return to my previous form. I am afraid that I must go now, but I want you to know how much your love has meant to me, both when I was a bird and when I was a child."

Tears welled up in the woodcutter's eyes, and his wife began to sob quietly. "Come," Megumi said. "I wish to be with you until the very last." The girl gestured for the couple to follow her. They headed for a broad field. Once there, Megumi said, "Close your eyes, and count to seven before opening them. Good-bye, my beloved ones. I shall always remember you."

"And we shall never, ever forget you. Good-bye, crane-child," said the woodcutter and his wife, kissing the girl tenderly one last time. Then they did as Megumi had asked, and when they opened their eyes they saw that the girl was no more. In her place stood a magnificent crane whose neck was proudly arched and whose feathers glistened like sunlit snow. The crane met their eyes, and held them in its gaze before bowing its head in mute acknowledgment. The woodcutter drew his wife to him as the crane bounded across the windswept field, gaining enough speed to send it aloft. They watched in silence as the bird rose into the sky, growing smaller and smaller as it was swallowed by the distance.

a tale from Japan
retold by Susan Milord
From *Tales Alive! Bird Tales from Near & Far*

Far Up the River

A PAIR OF GOLDEN ORIOLES
Sings in the bright green willows.
A line of white egrets crosses
The clear blue sky. The window
Frames the western mountains, white
With the snows of a thousand years.
Anchored to the pilings are
Boats from eastern Wu,
Three thousand miles from home.

—Tu Fu

Eastern Wu, the lake region of what was then Southern China, seemed, and still seems, a paradisal region to the Chinese.

Brimming Water

UNDER MY FEET THE MOON
Glides along the river.
Near midnight, a gusty lantern
Shines in the heart of night.
Along the sandbars flocks
Of white egrets roost,
Each one clenched like a fist.
In the wake of my barge
The fish leap, cut the water,
And dive and splash.

—Tu Fu

A Crossing South of Li-chou

TRANQUIL, VACANT *is the river, girdled by the setting sun;*
An island, vast, misshapen, merges with the flanking hills.
See, an oar is raised, a horse whickers across the waves;
By willow trees men rest, waiting the ferry's return.
From thick clumps of sand grass, seagulls flock, disperse,
While above endless fields along the river, a solitary egret
    rises.
But who will raise the sail in search of Fan-Li
Now oblivious to desire among the misty waters of Five Lakes.
                    —Wen T'ing-yun
                from *Sunflower Splendor,*
      Three Thousand Years of Chinese Poetry

Isaiah 38:14

LIKE A SWALLOW *or a crane I clamor,*
I moan like a dove.
My eyes are weary with looking upward.
O Lord, I am oppressed; be thou my security!
          Holy Bible – Revised Standard Version

Spending the Night at a Mountain Temple

A HOST OF PEAKS REAR UP *into the color of cold,*
At this point the road splits to the meditation hall.
Shooting stars pierce through bare trees,
And a rushing moon retreats from moving clouds.
Visitors come but rarely to the very summit;
Cranes do not flock together in the tall pines.
There is a monk, eighty years old,
Who has never heard of what happens in the world.
                    —Chang Yu
                from *Sunflower Splendor,*
      Three Thousand Years of Chinese Poetry

How Crane Got His Long Legs

I N THE DAYS OF THE Grandfathers, Rabbit thought to himself, I should like to ride on the moon. Rabbit looked at the full moon as it came up from the edge of the eastern sky. He watched the moon go up in the sky above him. He watched the moon move across the night sky. Rabbit watched the moon until day came and he could not see the moon any longer.

"If I stand on the high hill at the edge the world," Rabbit said, "I will be able to get hold of the moon when it comes up."

That night Rabbit stood on the high hill. The moon came up slowly. It was so large in the sky that Rabbit reached out to touch it. He stood on his hind legs and reached for the moon. He stretched his front legs as far as he could to seize hold of the moon. The moon was too far away. It climbed into the sky and Rabbit watched it, but he could not reach it.

"I will get one of the birds to carry me to the moon," Rabbit said. He went to Eagle. "Carry me to the moon, Eagle," Rabbit said. "I want to ride on the moon, but I cannot reach it. I will pay you if you will take me to the moon."

No," Eagle said, "I cannot carry you to the moon. It is too far. I cannot."

Rabbit went to Hawk. "No," Hawk said, "I have other business to attend to. I cannot carry you to the moon."

Rabbit went to all the great flying birds. The great flying birds would not carry him to the moon.

Rabbit went to the small flying birds. The small flying birds laughed. "You are too big for us to carry you to moon," they said. "The moon is too far from the earth. No, we will not carry you to the moon."

Crane heard Rabbit. "I will try to carry you, Rabbit," Crane said. "Hold on to my legs, and I will see if I can fly with you to the moon."

Rabbit did as Crane said. Crane rose into the sky. Rabbit was heavy. Crane spread his great wings. It was all that Crane could do to fly with Rabbit. Rabbit looked down at the earth below. It was very small. It was very far away. Rabbit was not sure he wanted to ride on the moon. Rabbit's front legs ached. It was all that Rabbit could do to hold on to Crane, but he did.

Crane came to the moon. "Rabbit," Crane said, "I have done it."

Rabbit stepped on to the moon. Then he touched Crane's head. Crane's white feathers became red under Rabbit's hand. "This is my gift," Rabbit said. "From this day you will wear a headdress of red feathers."

So it was. From that day Crane has a red feather headdress, and his legs are long. They are longer than the legs of other birds. They were stretched from the weight of Rabbit when Crane carried him to the moon.

And if you look when the moon is full in the sky, you will see that Rabbit is still riding on the moon.

—Natalia M. Belting
from *The Long-tailed Bear and Other Indian Legends*,
a tale of the Cree Indians who live near James Bay and the Saskatchewan River in Canada.

Origami Crane Instructions

ORIGAMI, OR PAPER FOLDING, IS A popular pastime in Japan. Not surprisingly, one of the best-loved origami models is the crane.

For an origami crane, you will need a square sheet of lightweight paper, at least six inches in size.

CREASE SQUARE diagonally in both directions, then turn square over and crease in half both directions. (If using paper colored on one side only, begin with the colored side up.) ➤

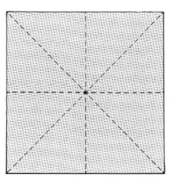

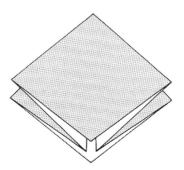

BRING FOUR corners together and press flaps down to form a square as shown in Fig. 2 ◄

FOLD CORNERS y and x to line a-b so that they meet in the center, at the crease. Fold down the top triangle along line a-b. ➤

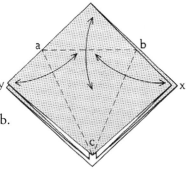

LIFT THE TRIANGLE at point c and unfold the folds you made in Step 3. Lift the top layer of paper upwards, pulling it so the outer edges come together. Press flat the diamond shape. Then turn the paper over and do the same with other side to make Fig. 5.

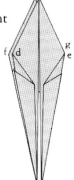

NEXT, FOLD SIDES in towards the center as shown in Fig. 5. Turn the paper over and repeat to make Fig 6.

BRING POINTS d and e together in front and f and g together behind to make Fig. 7. Press flat. ➤

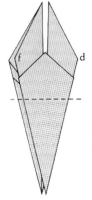

NOW FOLD UP along crease at dotted line, front and back to make Fig 8.

THEN BRING points f and d together in front and g and e together behind. Press flat. Pinch base with right hand while left pulls neck out slightly. Then pinch base with left hand while pulling out tail with right. Now fold down and pull out beak, pinching head. See Fig. 9.

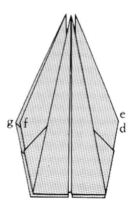

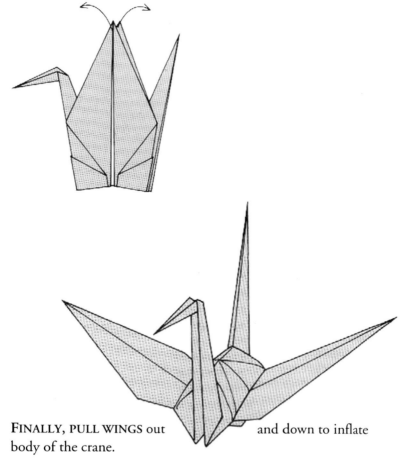

FINALLY, PULL WINGS out and down to inflate body of the crane.

The Crane Girl

YOSHIKO LIVED WITH HER parents in a village by the sea. In the mornings, she went for walks with her mother and found pretty pebbles on the beach.

In the evenings, she played with her father when he returned home from fishing. Soon there would be someone else to play with. Yoshiko's mother was going to have a baby.

It was exciting when the new baby arrived. He was tiny and soft and smelled like morning after the rain. Yoshiko's father named him Katsumi, and everybody loved him.

But now there were fewer walks with mother. All day long she was bathing and feeding the baby. Now there was not as much playing with father. He wanted to play with Katsumi too. Yoshiko began to think her parents no longer loved her.

The day her parents gave Katsumi his ormamori amulet to protect him from evil sprits, Yoshiko was jealous. It was made from the same cloth and had the same designs as the ormamori they had given her. Now she was certain she wasn't special anymore.

Yoshiko became more and more unhappy. She wanted to be a baby again. She was sure her parents wouldn't even notice if she went away. So Yoshiko walked through the misty morning toward the sea.

At the beach, she saw fish playing in the rippling water. *Pishan, pishan*, the fish splashed.

"Could I be one of you?" Yoshiko asked them. "Then I could be your baby and bathe with you. Then I would be happy." But the fish didn't answer, so she walked further.

In the forest, she saw monkeys swinging in the sunlit branches. *Kii, kii*, the monkeys chattered.

"Could I be one of you?" Yoshiko asked them. "Then I could be your baby and eat nuts with you. Then I would be happy." But the monkeys didn't answer, so she walked further.

On the hilltop, she saw a flock of dancing cranes. *Cur-lew, cur-lew*, the cranes cried.

"Could I be one of you?" Yoshiko asked them. "Then I could be your baby and dance with you. Then I would be happy." But Yoshiko was so tired from walking that, before the cranes could answer, she fell asleep in the tall, cool grass.

The cranes took pity on her, for she was such a lonely child.

"So be it!" said the leader. And together they swooped and whirled around her in a magical moonlit dance.

When Yoshiko awoke the next morning, she was a baby crane. All that remained of her human life was the omamori amulet her parents had placed around her neck for luck.

The cranes treated her like one of their own. They took her for walks and played with her and fed her mayflies with their beaks. As she grew older, they taught her how it was to fly, and they taught her to dance.

Yoshiko stayed with the cranes, and the seasons passed. But whenever she soared over the village by the sea, she remembered her family and wondered how they were.

Then one day Yoshiko decided to find out. She flew to her parents' house and perched high on a tree in the garden. There she overheard her mother and father telling a sad story to Katsumi.

It was about their precious first-born child, their beloved daughter, Yoshiko, and how they missed her.

Katsumi sighed and wished he had a sister to play with.

When Yoshiko saw how much her parents worried and how Katsumi needed a playmate, she wanted to be a girl again.

Cur-lew, cur-lew, she called, but they didn't understand. She leapt into the air and swooped to the ground. She bowed and stretched her wings.

She began to dance to show them she was well, but still they didn't recognize her. Tears sprang to her eyes. She whirled round and round until she was dizzy.

She jumped so high that she caught her wing on a branch and tore it badly. Then, hurt and exhausted, Yoshiko fainted and crumpled to the ground.

When Yoshiko opened her eyes, her family was leaning over her. Katsumi fanned her with a branch. Her mother tended the wounded wing while her father dripped cool water into her beak. Happiness filled her heart. For the first time in a long while, Yoshiko felt truly loved again.

As her mother gently stroked Yoshiko's feathers, her fingers closed around something familiar. A look of wonder appeared on her face. It was Yoshiko's omamori!

"Yoshiko?" she whispered.

At the sound of her name, the magic of the cranes ended, and Yoshiko became a girl again. Her parents were overjoyed to have her home, and she finally understood they had never stopped loving her.

In the days that followed, Yoshiko heard the cranes calling, *Cur lew, curlew.* And when she did, she would touch her omamori and remember how it was to fly.

Then she and Katsumi would dance together under the sky, to show the cranes she was happy.

—Veronika Martenova Charles

Omamori are good luck charms thought to bring good health, safety, and financial success. Though usually made of paper or wood, some, like Yoshiko's, are made of cloth. Omamori are sold by y priests at Shinto shrines and Buddhist temples. They are placed in family alters, doorways, fields, vehicles, or any place where extra protection might be desired. Omamori are also carried or worn about the neck as a more personal form of insurance against misfortune.

Onsongo and the Masai Cattle

The story so far is about Akinyi, a poor widow and a Kisii (an African mountain tribe near Lake Nyanza). She is traveling with her oldest fat, lazy son, Onsongo, and his two warrior brothers, Opio and Otinga, to the plains to raid forty cattle from the Masai tribe.

The cattle are to be used by Onsongo as a dowry to marry Anyika, a daughter of a wealthy Kisii tribesman. Being poor but an artist and thinker, Onsongo has carved an oxen-hunting horn to use in a plan to obtain the Masai cattle.

THE VERY NEXT DAY THEY set off for the plain, a day's hard walk away. They took with them enough food for a few days and a length of slender hide rope. The younger brothers carried hunting spears. Onsongo took his horn.

That night they slept on the top of the last steep slope that fell to the plain and in the morning when they had breakfasted on cold maize cake they moved along the hillside until they saw what they were looking for. Below them was a water hole, little more than a small pond in a sea of mud churned up by the feet of cattle and surrounded by dry reeds and a few trees. It was the end of the long dry season and water on the plain would be scarce. The marks of cattle were fresh; the Masai were using this pool.

However no one was there at the moment and Opio and Otinga went down to catch a crested crane, which was an important part of their plan.

They did it very neatly with a long noose made from the hide rope. They laid this out on the ground with a handful of grain scattered inside the noose for bait and then hid in the reeds with the free end of the rope. There were many cranes nearby, for in the dry season they stay close to water and when they saw the boys disappear into the reeds they came flying over to see what was happening. Cranes are as curious as cows about anything new going on.

Then one of them stepped with jerky strides into the noose and stabbed at the grain and Opio jerked the rope from the reeds and they caught him by his long nobbly legs. He lay on his back and screamed furiously: "Kerwonk!" and then they gathered him up and tied the wings and also put another piece of rope round that beak to stop him stabbing at them (a crane's beak is no joke).

Then they carried him up the hill and settled down in the grass to watch the water hole.

They were tired after their journey of the day before and under the hot sun they all fell asleep. When they woke it was late afternoon and the Masai had arrived. They counted ten young warriors, three standing on one leg apiece like storks, watching more than a hundred fine cows drink at the pool, the others lazing on their backs in the reeds or polishing their long spears with wisps of dry grass.

The four Kisii watched with their hearts beating faster. After the cows had been watered they crowded together near the water for the night. The Masai lit a fire and gathered round it, leaving two men to watch the cattle. The watchers guessed that what they were seeing happened every night.

In the morning the Masai drove the cattle across the plain out of sight but in a different direction from yesterday. When they were gone Akinyi and her three sons ate a little food and then they untied the crane's beak and gave the furious bird some food and water. After that they waited all day, but this time they were careful not to go to sleep.

When it was evening they saw, far away, a cloud of dust moving and this they knew was the cattle being driven back to water. Then all four of them slipped quickly down to where, a half a mile beyond the pool and on the other side of where the cattle slept, there was a solitary Mukubu tree, whose smooth gray bark was covered in long thorns. They helped Onsongo to climb this and when he was over the thorns they handed him up the tied crane and the horn. With these he disappeared into the dense leaves so that no one could have told a man was there. The other three went back to the pool and hid among the reeds.

The cattle came near and broke into a run when they smelled the water. Then the bellowing stopped as they reached the water. The Masai herdsmen followed. From close by they were a frightening sight; tall young men with faces like cruel masks and their hair arranged in plaits and dyed red. The long spears looked terrible. Opio, Otinga and Akinyi trembled and tried to forget all the shocking stories they had heard of the Masai. What Onsongo thought and how he behaved no one knows, because he was alone, but presently from the tree in which he was hidden there came the long hoarse roar of the horn. Onsongo blew it three times and finished the performance with a cluster of little graceful notes. Then there was silence.

The Masai pricked up their ears. They took their spears and leaving two of their number there lounged off round the pool and across the plain to where they judged the noise had come from. They were not suspicious, only idle and curious in a bored kind of way.

They were casting round rather like a pack of gaunt red hunting dogs when the horn blew again. It was a gentle sound now and almost seemed to talk. The Masai gathered at the foot of the tree and gazed up. There was nothing to be seen, no explanation at all of the noise.

They puzzled over it. One or two eyed the thorns lazily and decided against climbing up.

Their two companions at the pool called questions to them.

"Come and see," they shouted back from the tree and the two herdsmen glanced at the cattle. They were all drinking, soft noses lowered to the water, blowing quietly, mild eyes almost closed. They would finish drinking and then settle down where they slept each night. Nothing could happen. The two herdsmen skirted the reeds and joined their friends speculating beneath the trees.

As they arrived the horn blew again, three great blasts.

"It's a wizard," said the Masai.

"Nonsense, it's a bird."

"Oh, listen to the man. A bird! Whoever heard the like of that noise made by a bird?"

"It's Chemosit, Brother, who is half man and half bird. If we wait until night we'll see his mouth shining red." (Chemosit was a particularly unpleasant devil in whom the Masai believed.)

"Climb up there, Seriani. Climb up and tell us what it is."

"Not I. Not with Chemosit standing up there on one leg with his great mouth gobbling behind the leaves. Besides, the thorns are sharp."

The horn blew softly.

"Listen to it. Trying to tempt one of us up."

"Bah, that's neither a bird nor Chemosit. It sounds like a horn."

"Eh! Have you ever heard a horn blow itself?"

The horn howled harshly.

"There, listen to it. It's Chemosit and now he's angry because his plan has failed and no one has gone up."

And while they stood there, lazily babbling in the dusk, on the other side of the reeds, Opio, Otinga and Akinyi gathered together the cattle and, unseen, drove them away to the hills.

It was as easy as that.

From the tree Onsongo watched them go. He listened with half his mind to the Masai exercising their imagination below, the rest of him trying to judge the best time for the next move. His brothers and the cattle had now disappeared into the evening haze. They would be in the hills and with a long start. In half an hour it would be dark and impossible to follow them. Even if he could see their tracks, not even the Masai would go wandering at night through the Kisii hills after a raiding party whose size they did not know.

Onsongo decided that now was the time.

He blew his horn three times with all his strength. His brothers heard those notes distantly and knew what they meant. They hurried on, sweating, whispering to the cows and tapping their flanks gently with the butts of their spears.

Then, hidden by the leaves, Onsongo tied the horn to the leg of the crane, untied the bird's wings and beak and set it loose.

It jumped out of the leaves, flapped indignantly over the gaping Masai, the horn dangling from its leg. Then it opened its beak, shouted furiously, "Kerwonk!" and flew off clumsily.

The Masai stared after it.

"I said it was a bird!"

"Did you see the horn? That's no bird. It's a magician in the shape of a bird."

"And the horn's a magic horn!"

And they all set off like the wind across the plain after the crane to capture the magic horn, for the bird, hampered by the horn, kept landing and hopping round on one leg and then flying on, squawking.

The Masai chased it for a while before it vanished in the darkness. Then they came back to the pool and found every cow gone. Eh!

And of course while all this was going on Onsongo got out of that tree and ran to the hills as fast as his short fat legs would carry him. He wasn't built for running, but just then he had an excellent reason for it and he did quite well.

He joined his mother and his brothers in the hills and they reached home safely with more cattle than any of their neighbors had ever seen before.

And that is really the end of the story.

Onsongo married his Anyika and very happy they were, although sometimes she used to complain that he was lazy.

Then Onsongo would rouse himself and look at her indignantly.

"Lazy! Me? Bah, I was thinking. Thinking, woman! Do you know what that means? What I did when I got the cattle from the Masai. Brains are better than brawn any day!"

And he would stalk off and be found sleepily carving a piece of wood ten minutes later, his temper quite restored.

The crane? He flew to a tree for the night and the thong that held the horn broke and set him free. The horn lodged in the crook of a branch and the next year a tiny red-capped bird, whose name I have forgotten, made a nest inside and reared five splendid children.

As for Akinyi, she lived to be a hundred and nine and became the most famous old woman in the whole history of the Kisii tribe.

—Humphrey Harman
abbreviated from *Tales Told Near A Crocodile*
Stories from Nyanza, a province in Kenya,
Central Africa, on the eastern shores of Lake Victoria.

Living in the Hills

IN SOLITUDE I CLOSE MY WOODEN GATE,
As shadows fall I watch the setting sun;
The cranes have made their nests among the pines,
And to my rustic door few callers come;
Fresh powder dusts the young bamboo,
Its faded petals the red lotus sheds;
At the ferry landing lights spring up
And girls laden with water-chestnuts come flocking home.

—Wang Wei
from *Poetry and Prose of the Tang and Song*

HISABKO, A VICTIM OF THE ATOMIC bombing of Hiroshima, believed that if she made 1,000 origami cranes she would be healed. Although she died before meeting her objective, today the crane is a symbol of peace.

—George Archibald
Director, International Crane Foundation

Tower of the Yellow Crane

CHINA IS VAGUE AND immense where the nine rivers pour.
The horizon is a deep line threading north and south.
Blue haze and rain.
Hills like a snake or tortoise guard the river.

The yellow crane is gone.
Where?
Now this tower and region are for the wanderer.
I drink wine to the babbling water – the heroes
are gone.
Like a tidal wave a wonder rises in my heart.

(The Tower of the Yellow Crane is a high tower on a cliff west of Wuchang in the province of Hupeh. There is a legend that the saint Tzu-an once rode past the area on a yellow crane, thought to be an immortal bird. Another legend holds that Fei Wen-wei attained immortality immediately at this spot and regularly flew past on a yellow or golden crane. To commemorate these events a tower was erected and the place became a pilgrimage site for scholars and poets.)

—Mao Tse-Tung
Spring 1927
From *The Poems of Mao Tse-Tung*

Storks and Frogs

A FROG STARTED AN argument with a Stork.
"Which of us two is the handsomer?" asked the Frog.

"I am," said the Stork. "Look what fine legs I have!"

"But you only have two of them," said the Frog. "And I have four."

"Maybe I only have two," replied the Stork, "but mine are longer!"

"Yes, but I can croak, and you can't!"

"But I can fly, and you can only jump."

"Sure you can fly, but you can't dive."

"That may be, but I have a bill."

"Do tell! So you have a bill! But what is it good for?"

"Here's what it's good for!" said the angry Stork. And he promptly swallowed the Frog.

—Sergei Makhalkov
from *Let's Fight!: And other Russian Fables*

On an evening when the spring mists
Trail over the wide sea,
And sad is the voice of the cranes,
I think of my far-off home.

Thinking of home,
Sleepless I sit,
The cranes call amid the shore reeds,
Lost in the mists of spring.

—Otomo Yakamochi
from *The Manyosku: One Thousand Poems*
Poem links the melancholy cry of cranes
with loneliness in the human heart.

From *The Story of the Wind*

NEAR THE SHORES OF THE great Belt, which is one of the straits that connect the Cattegat with the Baltic, stands an old mansion with thick red walls. I know every stone of it," says the Wind. "I saw it when it was part of the castle of Marck Stig on the promontory. But the castle was obliged to be pulled down, and the stone was used again for the walls of a new mansion on another spot—the baronial residence of Borreby, which still stands near the coast. I knew them well, those noble lords and ladies, the successive generations that dwelt there; and now I'm going to tell you of Waldemar Daa and his daughters. How proud was his bearing, for he was of royal blood, and could boast of more noble deeds than merely hunting the stag and emptying the wine-cup. His rule was despotic: 'It shall be,' he was accustomed to say. Waldemar Daa and his wife had three children, daughters, fair and delicate maidens—Ida, Joanna, and Anna Dorothea, who are compared to a rose, lily, and hyacinth. I have never forgotten their names. They were a rich, noble family, born in affluence and nurtured in luxury.

"I returned again; I often returned and passed over the island of Funen and the shores of the Belt. Then I rested by Borreby, near the glorious wood, where the heron made his nest, the haunt of the wood-pigeons, the blue-birds, and the black stork. It was yet spring, some were sitting on their eggs, others had already hatched their young broods; but how they fluttered about and cried out when the axe sounded through the forest, blow upon blow! The trees of the forest were doomed. Waldemar Daa wanted to build a noble ship, a man-of-war, a three-decker, which the king would be sure to buy; and these, the trees of the wood, the landmark of the seamen, the refuge of the birds, must be felled. The hawk started up and flew away, for its nest was destroyed; the heron and all the birds of the forest became homeless, and flew about in fear and anger. I could well understand how they felt. Crows and ravens croaked, as if in scorn, while the trees were cracking and falling around them. Far in the interior of the wood, where a noisy swarm of laborers were working, stood Waldemar Daa and his three daughters, and all were laughing at the wild cries of the birds, excepting one, the youngest, Anna Dorothea, who felt grieved to the heart; and when they made preparations to fell a tree that was almost dead, and on whose naked branches the black stork had built her nest, she saw the poor little things stretching out their necks, and she begged for mercy for them, with the tears in her eyes. So the tree with the black stork's nest was left standing; the tree itself, however, was not worth much to speak of."

Over a disagreement over Waldmar Daa's proud black horses, the admiral did not buy the new ship for the king. It remained on the shore covered with boards—a Noah's ark that never got to the water—Whir-r-r-r—and that was a pity.

"In the winter, when the fields were covered with snow, and the water filled with large blocks of ice which I had blown up to the coast,'" continued the Wind, "great flocks of crows and ravens, dark and black as they usually are, came and alighted on the lonely, deserted ship. Then they croaked in harsh accents of the forest that now existed no more, of the many pretty birds' nests destroyed and the little ones left without a home; and all for the sake of that great bit of lumber, that proud ship, that never sailed forth. I made the snowflakes whirl till the snow lay like a great lake round the ship, and drifted over it. I let it hear my voice, that it might know what the storm has to say. Certainly I did my part towards teaching it seamanship."

"That winter passed away, and another winter and summer both passed, as they are still passing away, even as I pass away. The snow drifts onwards, the apple-blossoms are scattered, the leaves fall—everything passes away."

Waldemar Daa then began searching for gold by trying to make it from boiling, distilling, and mixing the stranges potions. But after numerous years he failed to discover the formula. Thus Waldemar Daa and his daughter became very, very poor and Borreby fell into disrepair. Waldemar Daa's enemy, Owe Ramel, of Basnas, had bought the mortgages and Borreby.

And what became of Waldemar Daa and his daughters? Listen; the Wind will tell us:

"The last I saw of them was the pale hyacinth, Anna Dorothea. She was old and bent then; for fifty years had passed and she had outlived them all. She could relate the history. Yonder, on the heath, near the town of Wiborg, in Jutland, stood the fine new house of the canon. It was built of red brick, with projecting gables. It was inhabited, for the smoke curled up thickly from the chimneys. The canon's gentle lady and her beautiful daughters sat in the bay-window, and looked over the hawthorn hedge of the garden towards the brown heath. What were they looking at? Their glances fell upon a stork's nest, which was built upon an old tumbledown hut. The roof, as far as one existed at all, was covered with moss and lichen. The stork's nest covered the greater part of it, and that alone was in a good condition; for it was kept in order by the stork himself. That is a house to be looked at, and not to be touched," said the Wind. "For the sake of the stork's nest it had been allowed to remain, although it is a blot on the landscape. They did not like to drive the stork away; therefore the old shed was left standing, and the poor woman who dwelt in it allowed to stay. She had the Egyptian bird to thank for that; or was it perchance her reward for having once interceded for the preservation of the nest of its black brother in the forest of Borreby? At that time she, the poor woman, was a young child, a white hyacinth in a rich garden. She remembered that time well; for it was Anna Dorothea."

"'O-h, o-h,' she sighed; for people can sigh like the moaning of the wind among the reeds and rushes. 'O-h, o-h,' she would say, 'no bell sounded at thy burial, Waldemar Daa. The poor school-boys did not even sing a psalm when the former lord of Borreby was laid in the earth to rest. O-h, everything has an end, even misery. Sister Ida became the wife of a peasant; that was the hardest trial which befell our father, that the husband of his own daughter should be a miserable serf, whom his owner could place for punishment on the wooden horse. I suppose he is under the ground now; and Ida—alas! alas! it is not ended yet; miserable that I am! Kind Heaven, grant me that I may die.'"

"That was Anna Dorothea's prayer in the wretched hut that was left standing for the sake of the stork. I took pity on the proudest of the sisters," said the Wind. "Her courage was like that of a man; and in man's clothes she served as a sailor on board ship. She was of few words, and of a dark countenance; but she did not know how to climb, so I blew her overboard before any one found out that she was a woman; and, in my opinion, that was well done," said the Wind.

Easter morning I heard the tones of a psalm under the stork's nest, and within the crumbling walls. It was Anna Dorothea's last song. There was no window in the hut, only a hole in the wall; and the sun rose like a globe of burnished gold, and looked through. With what splendor he filled that dismal dwelling! Her eyes were glazing, and her heart breaking; but so it would have been, even had the sun not shone that morning on Anna Dorothea. The stork's nest had secured her a home till her death. I sung over her grave; I sung at her father's grave. I know where it lies, and where her grave is too, but nobody else knows it.

"New times now; all is changed. The old high-road is lost amid cultivated fields; the new one now winds along over covered graves; and soon the railway will come, with its train of carriages, and rush over graves where lie those whose very names are forgotten. All passed away, passed away!"

"This is the story of Waldemar Daa and his daughters. Tell it better, any of you, if you know how," said the Wind; and he rushed away, and was gone.

—Hans Christian Andersen
Written 1859
Translated by Henrietta Nygaard Rasmussen

From *Tune: 'As in a Dream: A Song' Two Lyrics - #1*

HOW MANY EVENINGS IN THE arbor by the river,
when flushed with wine we'd lose our way back.
The mood passed away, returning late by boat
we'd stray off into a spot thick with lotus,
    and thrashing through
        and thrashing through
startle a shoreful of herons by the lake.

—Poetess Li Ch'ing-chao
from *Sunflower Splendor,*
Three Thousand Years of Chinese Poetry

Autumn Evening Beside the Lake

WIND PASSES OVER THE LAKE.
The swelling waves stretch away
Without limit. Autumn comes with the twilight,
And boats grow rare on the river.
Flickering waters and fading mountains
Always touch the heart of man.
I never grow tired of singing
Of their boundless beauty.
The lotus pods are already formed,
And the water lilies have grown old.
The dew has brightened the blossoms
Of the arrowroot along the riverbank.
The herons and seagulls sleep
On the sand with their
Heads tucked away, as though
They did not wish to see
The men who pass by on the river.

—Poetess Li Ch'ing Chao

A Parable

EAST OF THE RIVER THERE'S A FOUL BIRD
Which calls itself the bad pelican.
It feeds on fish, barely cramming its throat;
Its feathers are simply a disgrace.
That's why from the bank where it stands,
Gulls and egrets always fly far away.

Whence comes this grayish hawk,
With iron plumage and pupils flashing gold?
Though not at all elegant or refined,
Still it plots to swoop and strike.
It chooses not to soar high to the heavens,
But comes down, hovering over the cold river stream.
Sidewise, it edges to the pelican and eats its fill;
Then, spreading both wings, it flies off to roam the skies.

How could a lower stream become habitable?
Noble or base: each seeks what he will.
That's why the mind of an aged crane
Remains aloof and disdains the high autumn.

—Ch'en Tzu-lung
from *Sunflower Splendor,*
Three Thousand Years of Chinese Poetry
A bad pelican is a type of water bird, or bald crane, larger than a
crane and of dark gray color. It has a bald, red top, yellow beak, and
a pouch like a pelican's; it loves to feed on refuse, fishes, and snakes.

Part Six

Chirr-Bookie, the Blue Crane

CHIRR-BOOKIE WAS a Wimmera man. His sister, the only woman in his family, married into the Raminyeri tribe. This is how he became associated with the Raminyeri. He would often visit his sister, and he at last decided to live with his brother-in-law. Chirr-bookie's sister had three sons, and, like all uncles on the mother's side, Chirr-bookie delighted to take part in their education. They had to be instructed in hunting, fishing, bushcraft, and all the customs, traditions, and legends of the tribe. When the three boys grew up they received their names. The eldest one was called Eurowie because he was a great jumper, and was able to leap over obstacles like a kangaroo. The second was called Pithowie. He was not gifted as Eurowie was. He could not run or jump, but he was persevering, and was a good hunter in following game such as emus and wallabies. If a subject were in dispute Pithowie would always hold by his opinion. The youngest brother was called Koolatowie. This name means 'easy to bend.' yet he was strong if there arose a dispute among the brothers. Koolatowie would always willingly yield in order to avoid angry words that might lead to a quarrel. This won him the respect and love of his mother and father and his uncle Chirr-bookie and the tribe of the Raminyeri, but it made his two brothers hate him. They were always seeking a cause of quarrel with him, and this grieved their good old uncle Chirr-bookie, who at last summoned the chief and the elders in order to suggest that Eurowie and Pithowie should be sent to another tribe. This was agreed to, and it was decided to send both to make their homes with the Adelaide tribe. So a messenger was commanded to approach the chief of the Adelaide tribe to ask if he was willing to receive the two young men and their wives. When the brothers were told to the intention of their tribe to transfer them they vowed secretly to take the life of Koolatowie, and it was with the spirit of revenge in their hearts that they bade farewell to their mother, father, uncle, and brother, and set out on their journey to their new home, to begin life in a new country with new people who spoke a strange language.

After Eurowie and Pithowie had become conversant with the language of the Adelaide tribe, and could speak it fluently, they began to plan ways and means of being revenged. They tried to prejudice the other tribes against their father's tribe, but no one would think of going to battle against the Raminyeri, because they were a peaceful tribe, and were respected by all. Then the brothers thought of another plan; they suggested that as certain animals and birds were becoming scarce it would be well to station men at the boundary of their country, in order to prevent these creatures from departing and wandering away into the land of another tribe. This plan appealed to the Adelaide tribe, and all the hunters—men, women, and children—were told to help to carry it into effect.

Now Eurowie and Pithowie knew that emu food was much sought after by their uncle Chirr-bookie. It was his favourite dish, and his nephew Koolatowie would travel long distances and endure great hardship and face great danger to procure it. They therefore made a plan to prevent the emus from passing, and drove them down toward a peninsula formed by a river bending in its course to enter the sea.

Every day Koolatowie would rise early in the morning and set out in search of an emu, but he would return to his mother and uncle with the same story that there were no emu tracks. He could not understand this. After some time Eurowie and Pithowie sent a messanger to their aged uncle to inform him that emus were plentiful in their hunting-ground, and that at the next full moon they would send a nice fat one. When Chirr-bookie received this message he sat down and took from his *punauwe* (a kangaroo-skin bag) a stone pencil, and made some marks upon a smooth stick (a message-stick) about four inches long and half an inch wide. The message was that, although he loved the fat and flesh of the emu so much, he had vowed that he could not eat of it unless the bird had been caught, killed, and cooked in the earth oven by Koolatowie.

When the messenger returned to the brothers they were greatly annoyed with the message, because it upset their plans. That afternoon they took up their spears, left their homes, and went to the peninsula and caught an emu, and bound its legs and carried it back with them. Late in the evening they took it beyond the boundary to Horseshoe Bend, just across the river, and let it loose. They waited till they saw it recover itself and set off toward Aldinga. They followed it for a few miles, then turned back homeward, and reached their camp about midnight. Then they had a late meal. They rose next morning before the sun, and armed themselves each with a *wunde*, three *waddies*, and a *kanake*. When the sun rose they were at the Onkaparinga river. At Horseshoe Bend they speared a couple of fishes and lit a fire and cooked their breakfast. Now they felt refreshed, and ready to do battle should they be challenged for trespassing. They followed the track of the emu, knowing well that if it wandered toward Cape Jervis and Koolatowie saw it he would be sure to hunt it, and kill and cook it before taking it home to his mother and uncle.

During that same morning Koolatowie set out hunting. He scoured the hills and valleys in search of an emu. Suddenly he stopped with his eyes fixed upon the ground. A few paces away he saw the footprints of an emu, the object of his hunt. This sight caused his blood to course rapidly through his body, filling him with great excitement. He noticed the direction of the emu's tracks, so he ran on a course in the form of a crescent, knowing that this would bring him ahead of his prey, since the emu would continue in the direction in which it was going. Being a great hunter and well versed in the knowledge of how to hunt the emu, he waited at the head of the valley. He hastily plucked branches of shrubs and made them into a shield about three feet long and eighteen inches wide. He waited patiently.

It was some time before the emu came in sight. When Koolatowie saw it he took hold of his shield with his left hand and his spear with his right. The emu came on toward him, picking berries and young leaves from bushes and plants. As it approached Koolatowie would move in the line of its travel. When the emu moved to the left the hunter moved to the left, and when the emu moved to the right the hunter moved to the right. Nearer and nearer the hunter approached the prey, until he was within striking distance. He allowed the emu to pass about three yards away from him to the left, then he threw his spear and struck the bird in a vital spot. It dropped instantly. With a bound Koolatowie reached the side of the emu and removed the spear from the body, and allowed the blood to flow. He tied the two legs of the bird to its head and neck and then took the emu and lifted it up, and placed his head between the legs and neck, which formed a loop, and soon it was swinging over his shoulder with its legs and head to the side of his head. In this manner he carried the emu to the place where he meant to cook it, about a mile from where he had killed it.

When Koolatowie arrived at the spot he dug a hole and gathered grass and a few twigs and some strips of the bark of a dry she-oak log lying on the ground. Then he made a fire, and burned the bark till it made excellent coals. He placed some more bark in the hole, and he also threw a lot of small stones among the blazing wood. After the wood burned there was a layer of red coals and hot stones. Then he took small boughs of shrubs and placed them upon the hot stones and coals. Upon this he placed a layer of soft grass. After this he took up the emu with all its feathers on, and placed it on top of the grass. Then he put more boughs upon the emu, and covered the whole with earth, leaving only the head of the emu uncovered. On top of this earth he made a fire, and thus the emu was lying below the level of the surface of the ground, with only its head protruding. After this Koolatowie felt satisfied, and sat down and chanted songs of the hunter.

Now Eurowie and Pithowie, who had so often hunted with their uncle, Chirr-bookie, knew that emus in this part of the country always travelled in a certain direction – via, southward – as if prompted by instinct, and that on their way they passed through a certain valley. The brothers made for the valley, and began looking about for the tracks of the emu. Pithowie found the tracks first, and called to his brother to come and look at them. They both followed the tracks until they reached the place where the emu was slain. Here they saw the blood upon the ground and grass, and they also saw the footprints of Koolatowie. They followed these tracks until they could smell the fire and the cooking. They walked boldly forward toward Koolatowie. Koolatowie rose to his feet with his spear in his hand fixed upon the throwing-stick, and stood on guard, ready to meet anyone who should come with unfriendly intentions. The brothers threw their spears upon the ground, and called, "Younger brother of ours, how do we see thee? There have been great changes, and many moons have passed. Do no hold back that brotherly feeling which belongs to us both. Give place to tears of joy and delight because we have come together after being long separated. Come, let us weep with one another!" So Koolatowie placed his spear upon the ground and beckoned that they should come forward and be seated beside him.

Eurowie and Pithowie came forward, and sat one on each side of Koolatowie. They began to inquire about their mother and father and their uncle Chirr-bookie. Then they asked about other members of the tribe. After some talk they told him how scarce emus were. They said they had seen the tracks of the one that

Koolatowie had killed, and they had followed it, hoping to caputure it, as they were anxious to taste the food. It was many moons since they had eaten emu-flesh. Koolatowie said, "O my two brothers, did you not send a messenger to Uncle some two moons back saying that if he would like an emu you would send him one? Is that so, or am I mistaken?" Then Pithowie answered, "Perhaps the messenger made a mistake. If emus were plentiful do you think we should dare to come over the boundary-line hunting one? But, brother, you have been lucky to capture this one. It has travelled through all the hunting-grounds of the tribes, where there are many expert hunters. You have therefore distinguished yourself as a great hunter."

Although Koolatowie had received a thorough training in hunting and bushcraft he was not acquainted with the subtle cunning of his brothers in using this weapon of flattery. It put him completely off his guard. Eurowie and Pithowie saw how their younger brother had fallen a victim to flattery, and without warning, and with the swiftness of well-trained and expert hunters, they seized their weapons. Eurowie struck Koolatowie across the forehead with a *kanake*, and Pithowie dealt him a blow on the same part, which rendered him completely unconscious. Then

Eurowie took up his spear and pierced Koola towie's heart, thus killing him. Eurowie and Pithowie took up the body and carried it down the valley to the place where the emu was killed. They dug a hole about three feet deep, and placed the body in it, and covered it with grass and boughs. Then they put earth over the top of all this. After they had done this they took up the emu and stole hastily away. They returned home to their families, and sat round the camp-fire and enjoyed a meal of the cooked emu.

At the moment that Koolatowie was killed Chirr-bookie felt that something dreadful had happened, and he was greatly distressed and began to weep. "Where, oh, where art thou, O nephew of mine?" he cried. "Something within me says that thou art no more." Chirr-bookie continued to weep and to repeat these words all the afternoon, until the setting of the sun. The mother and father of Koolatowie came round, and feeling uneasy, they asked Chirr-bookie why he was weeping. He told them, and they said they thought the boy would be all right. However, they waited up all night, thinking that Koolatowie would return; but when the sun rose they were still waiting. Then Chirr-bookie went to the beach, and plunged into the sea, and stayed under water for a minute. He then rose to the surface and swam ashore. When he came out of the water he shook himself and ran round several times. Then he leaped into the air with one arm stretched upward, and shouted out this challenge, "O nephew of mine, whoever has slain you will have to kill me, because I go forth to take revenge – an eye for an eye and a life for a life."

Chirr-bookie hastened to his camp, and made his preparations for a journey. He knew not what was before him. He sat down and broke his fast, eating fish and herbs. Then he rose to his feet and shouted out, with a loud voice, "I rise to go forth to avenge! I shall not return until I have killed those who have slain my nephew!"

He left his camp, well armed with two spears, six *waddies*, two *panketyes*, and a *kanake*. There was murder in the heart of Chirr-bookie. As he walked away it was noticed that he stepped out with the elasticity of youth. As is the custom when a person goes out to kill some one, Chirr-bookie left his camp without bidding anyone good-bye.

As Chirr-bookie went along toward Mount Barker he communed with the spirits, of whom there are many, and begged of them not to intervene in any way, but rather to withdraw their influence, as he wished to be avenged for the death of his nephew. So the spirit of the north wind stepped forth and blew with much force round the base of Mount Barker, then leaped to the top, where Chirr-bookie sat with his head bowed, and said, "O Chirr-bookie, I shall not intervene. My presence shall be withdrawn. Go and slay your enemies." The west wind, the east wind, and the south wind all spoke to him in like manner.

Once more Chirr-bookie offered a prayer to the spirit of life. And the Father of All came out of the Milky Way with such tremendous force that he rent the air like lightning, causing a noise greater than many thunderbolts. He stood beside Chirr-bookie and asked him to rise. Chirr-bookie rose, and covered his face with his hands. He said, "O Father of All Spirits, grant me my requests. I ask that thou wilt withdraw thy presence and thy influence from Eurowie and Pithowie because they have slain one of thy beloved sons, Koolatowie, a young man who feared thee. I wish to take their lives and the lives of their wives and families. Then after I have slain them I do not wish that they should live an active life, but that they should become earth. Even then my spirit of revenge will not be satisfied; but I shall continue to kill every being that I meet on my way home who refuses to help me. O Father, let the spirits of those that I kill live in the form of birds, and when I die permit me to be changed after the same fashion." The Father of All Spirits answered, "O my son, thou child of my desire, go and do as thy conscience bids thee, and it shall be as you wish." So Chirr-bookie hastened on to fulfill his desire, and he came to Mount Torrens. Once more he prayed, asking the spirits of weapons to guide and give accurate flight to the boomerang, the spear, and the *waddy*. From out of the trees from which weapons were made came the answer, "We come to do thy bidding, O Chirr-bookie."

Chirr-bookie went straight from Mount Torrens to the home of Eurowie and Pithowie. He arrived just as the sun sank in the western sky. Upon his face and body there were signs painted showing that he had been on a very long journey and was just returning home. This gave the impression that he was not aware of the death of Koolatowie. When he met Eurowie and Pithowie they began asking him questions regarding the health and well-being of their mother and father. They asked how Koolatowie was when Chirr-bookie left home. The old man said that every one was well and happy at the time of his setting out on his journey.

Now Eurowie and Pithowie held secret converse, planning to take the life of Chirr-bookie. They invited Chirr-bookie to stay in their big camp; but he refused, choosing rather to sleep behind some bushes about a quarter of a mile away. Then they all retired in order to rest their weary bodies. At midnight Chirr-bookie rose and set fire to the camp of Eurowie and Pithowie; and the spirit of fire consumed Eurowie, Pithowie, and their families.

The old man wept bitterly for his two nephews, because he still loved them after a fashion, and he cried, "O my children, sons of my only sister, it is because of what you have done that the anger of all the spirits and gods has punished you."

Chirr-bookie then set out on his journey homeward, and at Aldinga he met a man of the Hawk totem tribe, who was fishing. The Hawk man sat with his eyes gazing seaward. Chirr-bookie called to him, and said, "O cousin, have you any fish to offer me?" The Hawk man would not answer, so Chirr-bookie threw his *waddy* at him with such force that it killed him instantly. Then he called out, "O cousin, thy body shall become a stone, and thy spirit shall take unto itself the body of a bird."

Chirr-bookie continued on his journey till he came to Yanka-lilla. Here he saw a man of the Shag totem, sitting up and sunning himself upon a rock. "O cousin of mine," said Chirr-bookie, "give me fish to eat." But the Shag man took no notice. So Chirr-bookie threw his *waddy* at him and killed him. Like the man of the Hawk totem tribe, his body became a stone, and his spirit took the form of the body of a bird.

When Chirr-bookie reached his home he took the remains of Koolatowie into a cave and placed them upon a ledge, and stretched himself out beside them. He prayed to the Father of All Spirits to come and transform him into a blue crane, and to call back the wandering spirit of Koolatowie and command it also to become a crane. The spirit came and sang a song that belonged to the Spirit World, and the body of Chirr-bookie became a stone man, which is still to be seen, and his spirit entered into the body of the blue crane.

The story of Chirr-bookie is intended to educate the Raminyeri or other tribes in a belief in the reincarnation. Chirr-bookie was the name of a person belonging to the Raminyeri tribe who was greatly respected by his own and other tribes. He was a good-living man, and he taught the people that if they fulfilled the laws and customs they should, if they so desired, could continue to live on the earth. If death came to them by accident, or in warfare, or by a pointing-bone, or by any other such means, they would only have to wish and that wish would be granted. If, however, a person was a law-breaker, and a good man killed him, the good man could express a wish that the bad man should become a stone. Upon wishing the bad man would become a stone.

—W. Ramsay Smith
from *Myths & Legends of the Australian Aboriginals*

Nurunderi's Wives

A NOTHER AUSTRALIAN Aborigine folklore tells of "blue crane" being a keeper and is in charge at the mainland end of a strip of land that reaches to the Spirit Land. "No one would attempt to cross without blue crane's permission. He was an austere person, and one with whom it was decidedly dangerous to dispute, because he always had beside him a very sharp-bladed spear, that would cause an exceedingly severe wound."

—W. Ramsay Smith
from *Myths & Legends of the Australian Aboriginals*

Lieh Mountain

THE RED WALLS OF THE old temple emerge from the blur of
the blue-green mountain;
Water from the lichen- and moss-covered precipice
spatters our clothes.
A formation of white herons takes off and rushes at our boat,
And then flies to the top of a pine tree halfway up the cliff.

—Wang Shih-chen
from *Sunflower Splendor*,
Three Thousand Years of Chinese Poetry

Crane

PRINCESS NAMIREMBE of Uganda sits in her father's great canoe.
Listen to the men who paddle:

"We are taking our Princess to the Island of Sese
Where the sands are smooth and bright,
The forest deep and dark,
And the valleys cool and green.

"See our paddles dive into the water,
See our paddles fly out of the water,
See our paddles shoot through the air."

Princess Namirembe of Uganda sits in her father's great canoe,
longing to travel farther than the Island of Sese. Listen to her father, the King:

"Wait, my daughter,
Wait, watch, and learn before you travel
To places far and wide where the ways are strange."

Princess Namirembe of Uganda picks fruit in her father's garden.
Listen to the crane:

"Oh, Princess, come,
Come to Kavirondo,
Far away over the great lake
To the wild country where the ways are strange.

Pamela J. Jensen

"Come, sit on my back,
Hold onto my feathers-my wings will steady you—
And close your eyes; for if you fall into the great lake,
You will drown."

Now Princess Namirembe of Uganda sits on the crane's back.
Listen to the crane:

"We are high in the sky,
Above islands so small no one lives there
But for diver birds, making their nests among the rocks.
Nothing else but sky, water, and sun."

Princess Namirembe of Uganda waits in Kavirondo while the
crane flies off to visit his brother. Listen to the Princess:

"I see great dark hills
And a plain stretching farther than my eye can see.
Here I see warriors with helmets of cowrie shells,
Ostrich feathers, and beads painted white, yellow, and red.
White, yellow, and red beads on the women
From a village that hides behind a fence of high, hard wood.

"Here there are no green hills
As there are in my Uganda.
Here there are no green banana gardens,
No fruit trees, no grass, as there are in my Uganda."

Princess Namirembe of Uganda travels back to Uganda with the
crane. Listen to the Princess:

"Oh, Father, I am back in beautiful Uganda with its
     lovely islands
And ripe crops glowing pink in the setting sun.
Let me tell you, oh, Father,
Where the crane took me. The ways were strange,
And the land was flat and dry,
Not like here in Uganda.
Uganda, I will never leave again."

205

Princess Namirembe of Uganda sits with her father and the crane. Listen to her father:

"You, oh, crane, I must thank
For showing my daughter other places
That makes her happy to be here.
I have a gift for you,
A golden crest, dark at its root.
Take it and wear it wherever you go."

Listen to the storyteller tell you:

"Look now at the crane and see his golden crest, dark at the root.
Look now at the crane and see his golden crest, dark at the root."

—Michael Rosen
Copyright 1992, 1991
from *How the Animals Got Their Colors*
Reprinted with permission of Harcourt, Inc.

(This myth comes from Uganda, in the Lake Region of East Africa. Until the 1960s Uganda was part of a kingdom called Buganda. Kings of Buganda were thought to have superhuman abilities, such as the power to give the crane a crest. Myths were told in dance and song by the elders as the tribe gathered around a fire. A listener could journey far from everyday life into another world (as the princess does in this story) and return refreshed and happy. On Lake Victoria's southwestern coast there is a town called Nyamirembe, and on the lake's western side are the Sese Islands. The crowned crane is found in much of Africa on marshes, plains, lakes, and seashore. About three feet tall, it eats small animals, fruit, and roots.)

Pamela J. Jensen

The Luan Family Rapids

IN SPATTERING AUTUMN RAIN
Over the rocks the swirling rapids plunge;
The leaping water sprinkles all around,
Startled into flight, the white egret alights again.

—Wang Wei
from *Poetry and Prose of the Tang and Song*

Climbing the Hill of Kami

CONTINUOUSLY, AS THEIR NAME TELLS,—
The tsuga trees that grow in luxuriance
With five hundred boughs outbranching,
On Mount Kamunabi of Mimoro—
And as endlessly as the creeping vine,
I would visit these ruins
Of the Palace of Asuka.
Here the hill is high, the river long;
On the spring day the hill is sweetest,
The stream is limpid of an autumn night,
The cranes wing the morning clouds in flocks,
The frogs call in the evening mists;
Whenever I gazed upon them
I am bowed in tears,
Remembering the days of old.

—Yamabe Akahito
Early to Middle Nara period, 710-784 AD
From *The Manyosku: One Thousand Poems*
Poem compares the association of cranes
with the beauties of nature.

WHILE STAYING IN A COUNTRY house in an empty woods, how could one go a single day without the company of this refined friend (the crane) that makes one forget all worldly things?

—Robert H. van Gulik
from *The Lore of the Chinese Lute*
from *Tsun-sheng-pa-chien,* a Chinese lute book

From *Crane Morning*

H E WAS ALONE NOW and in that fact also there was solace. He straightened himself and became aware of the cranes. Instantly delight leaped up in him, a flame of pure joy that burned against the habitual sadness of his thoughts much as the white cranes' wings shone against the sunless landscape. Seen from this distance, the flight of the cranes was the perfection of beauty and his joy that leaped to meet it was equally perfect.

...The laughter and the song were distant; what was near was the voice of the water about the piers of the bridge and the snap of the cranes' wings all about him. They were silent now, weren't cranes always supposed to be silent? Those that were over the river were dipping and wheeling and soaring silently, those in the fields were facing into the wind and gliding along as though the ridges of the plowed land were the waves of an inland sea. Against the deep brown of the turned earth their wings gleamed like snow—snow that was a little dirty, as when a salt plow has been over it; and when he looked up he could see clearly the grey feathers among the white, that same exquisite mother-of-pearl grey of the sky. And their flight! The freedom that was in those sweeping curves.

...Far above him the cranes were filling the sky with their excitement.

—Indrani Aikath-Gyaltsen
abbreviated from *Cranes' Morning*

(Chung-lu) Tune:
'Joy All Under Heaven'
(P'u-t'ien lo)
Sunset on the Western Hill

EVENING CLOUDS DISPERSED,
Setting sun hanging in the sky,
A stream of maple leaves,
And two banks of reed flowers,
Where gulls and egrets perch,
And oxen and sheep come down the road.
Ten thousand acres of gleaming water, as in a heavenly picture
Crimson clouds are immersed in the chill of the depths.
Congealed mist, twilight scene,
Flickering sunlight, ancient trees,
And dark shadows of crows flying away.

—Hsu Tsai-ssu
from *Sunflower Splendor,*
Three Thousand Years of Chinese Poetry

The Turtle and the Storks
And the Jackal

NEAR A VILLAGE ONCE in the long, long ago there was a pond at the edge of which lived two storks. They lived on the small fish which they caught daily in the pond.

But one year there was a long drought so that the water in the pond became less and less.

When the storks had eaten all the fish and saw the pond would soon be dry, one of them said to the other, "There are no more fish for us to eat. We are not so attached to this one place. Let us go to another place where we can find a pond with water."

The other stork said, "That is a good idea. Let us go at once."

So the two storks prepared to leave the pond at the edge of the village. Now there was also a turtle who lived in that pond. He overheard what the storks said and came to them, saying,

210

"Friends, I too have lived in this pond for a long time, and now that it is drying up, I too will have nothing to eat or water to live in. If you are going to another village where there is a pond full of water, will you not take me with you?"

One of the storks looked at him and said, "You foolish turtle, you cannot fly. You cannot go with us to another village."

The turtle looked up at them and said, "Ah, friends, it is true that I cannot fly, but surely you two storks can think of some way to get me there."

So the storks talked it over for a long time. Then they said to the turtle, "If you can close your mouth and keep it shut without speaking for as long as we are carrying you, we will take you to another pond."

The turtle assured them that he could close his mouth and keep it shut tight and never say a word during the flight to the other pond.

Then the storks brought a stick to the turtle and said to him, "Grasp the middle of this stick with your mouth, and hold onto it tightly during our flight. Never let go. Then we can carry you to the other pond."

The turtle grasped the stick firmly in his mouth.

Each stork grasped an end of the stick with his toes, flapped his wings, and rose into the air. As they were flying over a wide field, a jackal saw the shadow of the two storks carrying a turtle.

"What are you two doing, carrying a turtle through the air? He must be a very troublesome companion."

This made the turtle very angry, and he called down, "The troublesome companion is thirsty. They are kindly taking him to a pond which still has water." Having opened his mouth, the turtle lost hold of the stick and fell to the ground. He landed on his back, which cracked in all directions!

They say that this is how it happens that all the descendants of that turtle have cracked backs.

> a Ceylon folktale
> retold by Ruth Tooze
> from *Three Tales of Turtle:*
> *Ancient Folk Tales from the Far East*

Of Cranes and God

I RACE TO THE MAILBOX
On this bright spring morn,
And overhead I hear
The cry of the cranes
Northward bound.

I lift my eyes to scan the dreamy blue of sky
And there they are, drifting in the currents,
Now circling, now glistening in the sunlight
Sometimes looking almost white.

Into the house stuffy I plunge
To gather up my young son
So he too may witness
This Spectacle in the Sky.

Wave after wave pass by
Their reedy voices filling the gentle air.

Too long Winter has held us in his grasp,
Now surely the cranes can't be wrong.
Surely he wouldn't send his icy hand
To crush them in the northland!

I wonder how many are young—
This their first northward flight
And how many are old and wise,
Knowing the landmarks well.

Sometimes a solitary cry drifts down to earth
Not blending with the chorus.
Is he talking to us?

Poor land chained souls are we
Never to know the feeling of soaring high
Above trees and rivers and plains.

But thank you God
For ears to hear and eyes to see
These legions passing by
These legions in the sky.

All morning long they pass,
Some voices dying out
Only to be replaced
By new voices from the south
And always ever northward.

Where will darkness find you tonight, my friends?
I hope it's friendly lands.
So many things I wonder,
But all I can do
Is wish you luck and gentle winds.

—Valerie Vierk

From *The Girl from Flower Mountain*

THE JADE EMPEROR NODS HIS HEAD
   allows her return
riding dragons mounting cranes
   she reaches the blue void
Young lords of noble houses
   know little of the tao
come circling a hundred turns
   with ceaseless feet
Clouded windows misted belvederes
   these enraptured affairs
double-folded kingfisher curtains
   deep golden screens
The immortal ladder is hard to climb
   worldly ties are heavy,
idly they trust the blue birds
   to carry their youthful regards

—Han Yu
Translator Professor Charles Hartman
from *Sunflower Splendor,*
Three Thousand Years of Chinese Poetry

From *Tune: 'Greeting the Immortal Guest' Eight Songs - #7*

GATHERING SIMPLES, GOING HOME
white clouds flying
mist seals green mountains

and this wandering mystic's straight astray

black apes call and green birds cry
a magic crane goes before me, dancing
leads me to my cave.

—Yun-k'an Tzu
from *Sunflower Splendor,*
Three Thousand Years of Chinese Poetry

214

One Hundred and One Cranes

NOVEMBER LATE AFTERNOON, CLEAR, CHILL.
The sounds resonant from above, calling, calling.
V-shaped patterns circling, dissolving and merging
High, so high the eyes must squint to see.

In the blue, surrounded by abstract forms of clouds
Stark forms and black tipped wings, necks outstretched
Calling, calling to each in the group, south, south
Fly on to rest and food.

Why did I count, why was it so important?
The numbers change at our whim,
Forgotten, then remembered.
Hunted, then protected.
One hundred and one, I wish you speed to safety.
Winter home.

—Jessica Lyn Elkins

OUR APPRECIATION OF the crane grows with the slow unraveling of earthly history. His tribe, we now know, stems out of the remote Eocene. The other members of the fauna in which he originated are long since entombed within the hills. When we hear his call we hear no mere bird. We hear the trumpet in the orchestra of evolution. He is the symbol of our untamable past, of that incredible sweep of millennia which underlies and conditions the daily affairs of birds and men.

—Aldo Leopold
A Sand County Almanac New York, 1949
from *NEBRASKAland* magazine's
"The Road Home, A Photographic Journey"
with permission of Oxford University Press

From *Tune: 'Joy of Eternal Union'* (Yung-yu lo) Passing the Seven-League Shallows

A LEAF OF A LIGHT BOAT,
A pair of oars startling the wild goose –
   Pure water and sky,
   Clear shadows, calm waves –
Fish gambol and play among the mirrored water grass,
And egrets dot the misty riverbank;
I pass by a sandy brook, fast-flowing,
   A frosted brook, cold,
   A moonlit brook, bright.

—Su Shih
from *Sunflower Splendor,*
Three Thousand Years of Chinese Poetry

Egrets

IN CLOAKS OF SNOW, hairs snow-white, and beaks of blue jade,
They gather to hunt for fish, their reflection in the brook;
Startled they fly off, cast their distant shadows on green hills.
And all the blossoms of a pear tree fall in the evening breeze.

—Tu Mu
from *Sunflower Splendor,*
Three Thousand Years of Chinese Poetry

Lament of Hsi-Chun

About the year 110 BC, a Chinese princess named Hsi-Chun was sent, for political reasons, to be the wife of a central Asian nomad king, K'un Mo, king of the Wu-sun. When she arrived, she found her husband old and decrepit. He saw her only once or twice a year, when they drank a cup of wine together. They could not converse, as they had no language in common.

MY PEOPLE HAVE MARRIED ME
In a far corner of Earth:
Sent me away to a strange land,
To the king of the Wu-sun.
A tent is my house,
Of felt are my walls;
Raw flesh my food
With mare's milk to drink.
Always thinking of my own country,
My heart sad within.
Would I were a yellow stork
And could fly to my old home!

translated by Arthur Waley
from *A Hundred Seventy Chinese Poems*

The Geese and the Cranes

SOME GEESE AND CRANES were feeding together in the same field one day, when a bird-catcher suddenly came upon them. Since the cranes were slim and light, they could fly off right away and escape the bird-catcher's nets. The geese, however, weighted down by their fat, could not take off so easily and were all captured.

Moral: Those whom are caught are not always the most guilty.

—Aesop's Fables

Brokenleg Crane

The Nature Story: The Beginning

THE YOUNG CRANE followed the flock, circling slowly over the golden brown field. The refuge of the protected riverside was left miles behind in the breaking muted light of a cold dawn. The twelve birds were intent on the feeding for the day and had flown over the cornfield in days past. Yet today, the field looked different. Wide swaths of corn had been cut on one side of the field. Corn stalks lay broken and exposed on the ground with heavy ears of corn fallen in haphazard patterns. Loose corn from broken ears littered the dry winter earth. The older lead cranes circled in great arcs downward, each throat sounding their peculiar call to the others. This was a safe place to feed as the cranes could land in the open areas away from the thick erect rows of corn that might hide the predator. Young crane followed with outstretched wings, legs trailing behind until the last moment of descent. Dropping awkwardly without the experience of years of corn field cruising, young crane careened into another larger crane that immediately flapped his large gray wings and lunged at the younger bird. Youth must make mistakes to learn proper landing procedures, especially in crane flocks. Youth must be reprimanded by the elder. Gabbling, hopping, calling, scratching, fluttering, stretching all began at once among the flock. The skies resounded with more calls of incoming cranes, small groups of five, thirteen and twenty began arriving at the newly cut field until at last two hundred and four sandhill cranes dotted the field, thronging together for the great feast. From a distance the dusky gray bodies looked like clumps of thick smoke, swirling and bobbing. It appeared as if the bodies were magically suspended from the ground, so slight and spindly were the pairs of crane legs, supporting the heavy bodies. The birds' long thin necks swayed slowly forward in syncopation with the slow swaying walk that preceded finding just the right spot to dip the head and snatch a golden morsel from the ground. Young crane had never been in such a glorious feeding. Corn for the flock was spread before them like scattered jewels in the early light.

The feeding continued for several hours, first with much noise and flapping, but slowly taking on the appearance of a stately banquet. The party becomes more decorous as the belly is filled. Birds began picking more slowly and edging out into the perimeters of the mown area, searching for easy to reach kernels. Young crane has eaten well in spite of having to compete at times and losing to older more aggressive cranes who have been to such a laden field before. Eventually, small groups of cranes begin the fly away to the west, seeking the respite of river resting site. The young crane flapped his wings and departed with a group of thirty, flying low over the field just brushing the top of an ancient cottonwood. The young bird slowly ascended, but not quickly enough to miss the nearly invisible line stretched from pole to pole just behind the large tree. As the other cranes soared quickly upward, the young crane, laden with a heavy belly, dipped into the high wire. His left leg was struck with a glancing blow. The pain was intense and the crane faltered midair, only to recover in time from tumbling into wide empty irrigation drain below. The leg fell crookedly under his body. He was not able to thrust the leg back in the usual flight pattern.

Flapping frantically to keep up with the disappearing flock ahead, young crane felt the pull of the wounded leg dragging in the air under his wings. With all his might young crane continued to follow the flock until the river was in sight. Circling in behind the other birds, the bird faced the prospect of a water landing, but with only one stable leg. Dropping the right leg into a landing position beside the tangling left leg, the bird plummeted quickly from the sky, hopped onto the right leg just before the injured left leg gave way and jolted the bird head first into the soft sand of the marshy bar. He stood painfully, balanced on the good right leg while the bad left leg flamed with pain. An injured leg for a crane means a battle against all odds to take off in flight or land. An injured leg to a crane means difficulty in daily feeding, the stately crane walked off balance. Night fell for the flock by the river as young crane stood in pain, carefully moving from time to time and feeling the dull throbs radiating up and down the thin leg. The next dawn would begin the challenge of survival with pain.

The Watching Woman's Story

I SAW YOU FLY IN WITH two other cranes. The larger cranes were in perfect flight formation, but then I noticed something unusual about your flight. Your left leg dangled awkwardly down, not tucked back like the other cranes legs while in flight. When you landed, your injury was apparent. A broken or injured left leg prohibited you from the smooth parachute type landing of your fellow cranes. You stumbled and almost fell completely forward as the injured leg collapsed upon hitting the earth. You hopped slowly up, balancing your body on the one strong right leg as the left leg barely touched the ground. You had come to feed with the hungry sandhill flock that had discovered the newly cut corn field. This was a corn field planned for your feast and benefit. Two days before the farmer had cut down one third of the field, leaving the golden ears of grain scattered. You might have fed in the field the day before and were returning for another day of corn heaven. I had never seen a wounded crane. My experience was with the morality of tiny baby finches fallen from a nest or half eaten fledging sparrows caught by my eager cocker spaniel, brought happily into the kitchen and deposited at my feet. I watched as you began feeding with the two other cranes in an old alfalfa area aside from the main corn field, close to the abandoned pump house. For some time the other two cranes pecked avidly at the weed and alfalfa stubble on the ground. I watched with sorrow as you stood for long periods of time. You would peck at the ground under your legs and then hop awkwardly and painfully, wings flapping slightly, to another small area close by. The vast corn feast lay a field away. As larger groups of cranes began landing in the corn field, the two healthy cranes suddenly flew off to join the big flock, leaving you behind.

As I watched that day you stood alone feeding slowly, standing at alert to eye me occasionally as I stood on the rutted road, silently watching your sad plight. You fed in that small area for about an hour.

With great effort, many stilted hops and great flapping you then flew from your isolated splendor and circled to join the quiet larger crane flock. I lost sight of you among the busy, bobbing bodies of the feeding mass. Only once on my slow walk past the field did I think that I saw a crane pitch forward and almost fall when trying to reach a prize morsel of corn just out of reach.

I wondered about a wounded crane. Can I call someone to try to catch you and tend to your leg? Would Wildlife Rescue be interested? How can a crane survive a broken or badly injured leg, especially now during prime winter feeding time? What would happen to this crane during the coming spring migration back north?

Each day for a week when the large flocks of sandhills descended on the field you came with the others. Often I would see you, flying in, leg dangling and landing in the same area by the old pump house. Did you feel safe landing in the same spot each day? I thought that a coyote or large dog could certainly reach you since you were so close to the road. But each day you stood in the ragged weeds and tangled grasses, slowly feeding by yourself as the other cranes were in the bigger flock almost out of sight. Each morning I would hurry to see if you were still there, still upright, still feeding in your painful dance, the injured leg buckling under you with each attempted step. For seven days you were there, alone, isolated from the others. I never again saw you join the flock. Another neighbor had called the ranger to report a wounded crane, but when the ranger arrived you had gone. When I called Wildlife Rescue, the very concerned voice at the other end told me that this was nature's way. She explained that to try to catch the crane would probably be unsuccessful or cause greater trauma. Injured cranes have a chance to survive if they can fly. Only if the crane was actually lying on the ground, unable to fly should I call again, thank you very much. Now I knew I was only to wait and observe.

On the eighth day when I came to the pump house, the only thing in sight was a sad empty brown space. I scanned the other cranes nearby. I sat and watched for a long time trying to see if a broken leg crane was in the flock. Had you recovered from your injury? Did the time of isolation help you to heal? Could you now successfully take off in flight without the painful flapping and hopping? After seven more days of waiting for the sight of "Broken Leg," I despaired of seeing you again. The crane flock was decreasing each day as the great corn feast was eaten. Every morsel gone. Every cob picked clean. Scattered groups of four or five cranes now patrolled the edges of the field, looking for one last delightful taste. The broken leg crane never reappeared. I want to think that the injury was only superficial.

I want to believe that you healed before the long flight north. I want to hope that a hungry coyote didn't catch you during a time of rest back at the river or while you fed in the field. I dream of seeing you again next year in the great crane flock, strong, more mature, a crane that survived for another year of the endless cycle of migration and life.

The Nature Story: The Ending

FOR SEVERAL DAYS THE broken leg crane flew to the corn field with the larger flock, but always circled down to the same corner of the field by an abandoned pump house, close to the defunct irrigation ditch. He stood in the smaller area, away from the other cranes, eating small alfalfa sprouts and other vegetation that clung close to the soil. He was growing weaker from the efforts of having to hop painfully in small circles to forage. The pain in the damaged leg was constant.

The female coyote came from the bosque close to the big river. She often hunted in the large fields. The fields had changed. Corn had been planted where in the past the
land had been left fallow. Last year she had hunted mice, gophers, an occasional stray house cat. She had made many futile attempts to catch a large Canada goose, but had always failed. Now, something was different. Before her was a large flock of sandhill cranes, feeding on the vast corn field, bobbing, hopping, flapping. She began her slow, wary walk on the perimeter of the fields. She lowered herself into the tall brush and waited and waited. The coyote knew the game. She must look for a weak one, a young one, an injured one. An ill-timed pass within the view of the flock would cause the entire flock to take flight. She knew to wait and watch. Slowly she began a pattern of a large circle coming closer to the flock. Then she saw the isolated crane, standing a field away from the main flock. The crane was completely alone. The crane was pecking only occasionally at the sprouts in the hard earth. Tall brush and the empty, broken concrete irrigation ditch was close by. The coyote crouched even closer to the earth and changed directions. She began to slowly circle upwind from the lone crane. Padding stealthily behind the brush, she descended

into the shallow ditch hidden by the tall weeds between her and the crane. Now within a few yards, she suddenly leapt from the ditch and ran straight for the single crane. The crane started to hop in fear, tried desperately to take flight. Flight away from the predator, flight toward the flock. The injured leg would not give the crane sufficient time to soar away. Coyote was too quick. The crane turned sideways to encounter the snarling animal closing the distance between them. The crane stumbled over and fell off balance because of the wounded leg. The crane was down. Coyote viciously tore at the wing, then at the long slender gray throat as the crane with all his remaining strength tried to flap the once powerful wings. Two more brutal tearing bites, and the crane lay twitching and bleeding profusely from three fatal wounds. Coyote was quick to her work. This meant a large meal for the hungry belly. It was survival for another day.

Crane lay dying, strength ebbing away as coyote greedily tore at feathers and body. With one last shudder, the crane lay still. The broken leg was twisted beneath the warm gray body. The wings spread out from either side, in the pattern of desired flight. There was only one witness to the attack, a startled meadowlark, winging swiftly from his perch nearby.

The larger flock, now alert to the activity a field away, began departing in large groups. The sound of rushing wings and bodies, loud and measured honks, were a final song of farewell to the dead crane. The low sounds receded mournfully into the distance. The flock disappeared over the horizon, bound again for the safety of the river. The encounter, the hunt, was as nature intended. One gave life so another could continue life.

—Jessica Lyn Elkins
based on real life observations

Biographies of Writers and Artists

THE AUTHOR HAS MADE every effort to trace the ownership of all copyrighted material and to secure permission from copyright holders of such material. In the event of any question arising as to the use of any material the author, while expressing regret for inadvertent error, will be pleased to make the necessary corrections in future printings. Thanks are due to the following authors, publications, and agents for permission to use the material indicated.

Aesop, according to legend, was born either in Sardis, on the Greek island of Samos, or in Cotiaeum, the chief city in a province of Phrygia, and lived from about 620 to 560 BC. Little is known about his life, but Aristotle mentioned him acting as a public defender, and Plutarch placed him among the "Seven Wise Men." It is generally believed he was a slave, freed by his master because of his wit and wisdom. As a free man he went to Athens, ruled at that time by the tyrant Peisistratus, an enemy of free speech. As Aesop became famous for his fables, which used animals as a code to tell the truth about political injustice, he incurred the wrath of Peisistratus. Eventually Aesop was condemned to death for sacrilege and thrown over a cliff. Later, the Athenians erected a statue in his honor. In about 300 BC, Demetrius Phalereus of Athens made the first known collection of his fables, which then spread far beyond the Greek world.

Indrani Aikath-Gyaltsen lives in Darjeeling, India. She is a freelance journalist and has written short stories and one previous novel, *Daughters of the House.*

In 1942, **Lillian Amick** and her husband, Dr. Fred Amick, moved to the Platte River valley, south of Grand Island, Nebraska. They were amazed with the great flocks, thousands of birds, which flew to the river during spring migrations. "We were surrounded by them..." No one at that time seemed interested or was informed about the birds, especially the sandhill cranes. So Mrs. Amick researched the cranes, wrote an article, and the *Grand Island Independent* (newspaper) published it. It is gratifying to Mrs. Amick that in the 1990s the Platte River area is heavily traveled as visitors come to see the cranes and other birds arrive on their spring migration. She is 94 years old and stills feels that thrill when she sees and hears the cranes. Mrs. Amick is a member of the Nebraska Writers Guild.

Hans Christian Andersen, 1805-1875 AD, was a Danish poet, novelist, and writer of fairy tales. Reared in poverty, he left Odense at 14 for Copenhagen. He failed as an actor, but his poetry won him generous patrons including King Frederick VI. In 1829 his fantasy *A Journey on Foot from the Holmen Canal to the Eastern Point of Amager* was published, followed by a volume of poetry in 1830. Granted a traveling pension by the king, Andersen wrote sketches of the European countries he visited. His first novel, *Improvisatoren* (1835), was well received by the critics. His sentimental novels were for a time considered his forte. However, with his first book of fairy tales, *Eventyr* (1835), he found the medium of expression that was to immortalize his genius. He produced about one volume a year and was recognized as Denmark's greatest author and as a storyteller without peer. His tales are often tragic or gruesome in plot. His sense of fantasy, power of description, and acute sensitivity contributed to his mastery of the genre. Among his many widely beloved stories are *The Fir-Tree, The Little Match Girl, The Ugly Duckling, The Snow Queen, The Little Mermaid,* and *The Red Shoes.*

Dr. George Archibald was one of the two co-founders and is currently one of the Trustees of the International Crane Foundation headquartered in Baraboo, Wisconsin. He is considered the world's leading authority on cranes. Dr. Archibald was born July 13, 1946, in New Glascow, Nova Scotia, Canada. As a youngster, he had a keen interest in birds, and bred waterfowl, pheasants and chickens at home. One of his earliest memories, in fact, is of

crawling after a female duck and her brood. Later, during his undergraduate years, he spent two summers working as a bird care-
taker at the Alberta Game Farm, where he was introduced to
cranes. Dr. Archibald now lives in Baraboo, Wisconsin. Although
he is usually traveling four to six months a year, he enjoys gardening and is active in his church.

Lodovico Ariosto, 1474-1543 AD, was an Italian epic and lyric
poet. As a youth he was a favorite at the court of Ferrara; later he
was in the service of Ippolito I, Cardinal d'Este, and from 1517
until his death served Alfonso, Duke of Ferrara. He was never
properly rewarded by his patrons. While in the service of the cardinal, he began writing his masterpiece, the *Orlando Furioso*,
published in its final form in 1532. This epic treatment of the
Roland story, theoretically a sequel to the unfinished poem of
Boiardo, greatly influenced Shakespeare, Milton, and Byron. It
was intended to glorify the Este family as Vergil had glorified the
Julians. Ariosto also wrote lyric verse of unequal merit, but he was
among the first to write comedies in the vernacular (based loosely
on Roman models), among them *I Suppositi* (the pretenders) and
Il Negromante (the necromancer).

Basho, 1644-1694 AD, was a Japanese haiku poet, critic, and
essayist of the early Edo period. His literary name, Basho, is derived from the plantain trees (Basho) near a hut built for him by a
disciple. His later years were marked by several long and arduous
journeys that provided the basis for his famous travel accounts.
The *Oku no hosomichi* (narrow road to the interior), a reflection
in poetry and prose on his travel through the northern hinter-
lands, is considered his masterpiece. A student of Zen thought,
Basho played a central role in the development of the haiku verse
into a serious literary form capable of profound artistic expression. His poetry is particularly noted for its sensitive exploration
of themes relating to the nature of beauty, loneliness, suffering,
and death.

Don Brockmeier is a banker by profession whose hobby is nature
photography. His pictures showing nature's beauty, particularly
of birds and animals, have helped many individuals appreciate a

value they were unaware of. By motivating them he hopes to preserve the environment so others will have a chance to enjoy it. Don's photos have appeared in brochures promoting Central Nebraska. Other publication and catalogs have utilized his images showing rural life and nature. Don can be reached at 100 Johnson Place; Eustis, Nebraska 69028-0188.

Willa Cather, 1876-1947 AD, an American novelist and short story writer, born Winchester, Virginia, is considered one of the great American writers of the 20th Century. When she was nine her family moved to the Nebraska prairie frontier. She graduated from the University of Nebraska in 1895 and worked as a journalist and as a teacher in Pittsburgh. In 1904 she went to New York City. The publication of *The Troll Garden* (1905), her first collection of short stories, led to her appointment to the editorial staff of *McClure's Magazine*. She eventually became managing editor and saved the magazine from financial disaster. After the publication of *Alexander's Bridge* in 1912, she left *McClure's* and devoted herself to creative writing. For many years she lived quietly in New York City's Greenwich Village. The first of her novels to deal with her major theme is *O Pioneers!* (1913), a celebration of the strength and courage of the frontier settlers. Other novels with this theme are *My Antonia* (1918), *One of Ours* (1922, Pulitzer Prize), and *A Lost Lady* (1923). *The Song of the Lark* (1915) focuses on another of Cather's major preoccupations; the need of artists to free themselves from inhibiting influences, particularly that of a rural or small-town background; the tales collected in *Youth and the Bright Medusa* (1920) and the novel *Lucy Gayheart* (1935) also treat this theme. With success and increasing age Cather became convinced that the beliefs and way of life she valued were disappearing. This disillusionment is poignantly evident in her novel *The Professor's House* (1925). She subsequently turned to North America's far past for her material; to colonial New Mexico in *Death Comes for the Archbishop* (1927), widely regarded as her masterpiece, and to Seventeenth-Century Quebec for *Shadows on the Rock* (1931), in both novels blending history with religious reverence and loving characterizations. The volumes *My Mortal Enemy* (1926) and *The Old Beauty and Other* (1948) present her highly skilled shorter fiction. Her intense interest in the craft of fiction is shown in the essays in *Not Under Forty* (1936) and *On Writing* (1949). Cather herself was a master of that craft, her novels and stories written in a pellucid style of great charm and stateliness.

Isabelle C. Chang first heard many of the stories from her Chinese teacher when she was a child growing up in Boston. Years later, she wrote them down for her own children, filling in with her imagination when memory failed her. Mrs. Chang is a librarian with a bachelor's degree in library science from Simmons College and a master's degree in education from Clark University. She has worked in several libraries in Connecticut and Massachusetts, and at present is with the Shrewsberry, Massachusetts, Junior High School Library. She is married to Dr. M. C. Chang, a scientist, and has three children. Her other books include *Chinese Cooking Made Easy* and *Chinese Fairy Tales*.

Chang Yu, fl. 810 AD, was born either in Ch'ing'ho, Hopei, or Nan-yang, Honan, and was known primarily for his *yueh-fu* verses, many of which contain pointed references to contemporary or near-contemporary events and personalities. The poets Yuan Chen and Po Chu-yi had a low opinion of his works, which, however, won the praise of Tu Mu.

Veronika Martenova Charles, born in Prague, Czechoslovakia, was a popular music star in Eastern Europe before settling in Toronto, Canada, and became an illustrator of children's books. *The Crane Girl* is the first children's book she has written.

Geoffrey Chaucer, c. 1340-1400 AD, was an English poet, one of the most important figures in English literature. The known facts of Chaucer's life are fragmentary and are based almost entirely on official records. He was born in London between 1340 and 1344, the son of John Chaucer, a vintner. In 1357 he was a page in the household of Prince Lionel, later Duke of Clarence, whom he served for many years. In 1359-1360 he was with the army of Edward III in France, where he was captured by the French but ransomed. By 1366 he had married Philippa Roet, who was probably the sister of John of Gaunt's third wife; she was a lady-in-waiting to Edward III's queen. During the years 1370 to 1378, Chaucer was frequently employed on diplomatic missions to the Continent, visiting Italy in 1372-1373 and in 1378. From 1374 on he held a number of official positions, among them comptroller of customs on furs, skins, and hides for the port of London (1374-1386) and clerk of the king's works (1389-1391). The official date of Chaucer's death is October 25, 1400. He was buried in Westminster Abbey. Chaucer's final writing period, in which he achieved his fullest artistic power, belongs his masterpiece, *The Canterbury Tales* (written mostly after 1387). This unfinished poem, about 17,000 lines, is one of the most brilliant works in all literature. The poem introduces a group of pilgrims journeying from London to the shrine of St. Thomas a Becket at Canterbury. To help pass the time they decide to tell stories. Together, the pilgrims represent a wide cross section of Fourteenth Century English life.

Ch'en Tzu-lung, 1608-1647 AD, a native of Hua-t'ing (near Sung-chiang), Kiangsu, was poet, essayist, and patriot. Recognized as a skillful writer of the parallel-style prose, he was also noted for both his *shih* and *tz'u*. He was the compiler of a critical anthology of Ming poetry and another large volume of essays and memorials presented to the throne during the Ming dynasty.

Ch'u Yuan, 343? –278 BC, was China's first major poet. Besides being a poet, Ch'u Yuan was known as a virtuous statesman loyal to the king and patriotic to his country. A descendant of the noble family of Ch'u, he attained in his youth a high position at court and was entrusted with the compilation of government edicts and regulations. Throughout his long life Ch'u Yuan was so overwhelmed with grief and disappointment that shortly after the capture of the Ch'u Capital (Ying) by the Ch'in forces, he drowned himself in the River Mi-lo.

Claudius Claudianus, c.370-c.404 AD, was considered one of the last great poets of ancient Rome and was the last notable Latin classic poet. Probably born in Alexandria, he flourished at court under Arcadius and Honorius. Besides panegyrics, idylls, epigrams, and occasional poems, he wrote several epics, the most ambitious of which is the *Rape of Proserpine*, perhaps inferior to his epic attack *Against Rufinus*. Claudius has been highly regarded as a vigorous, skillful, and imaginative writer.

St. Columba, 521-597 AD, was born in Ireland where he is venerated for his work in founding monastic schools. He sailed to Scotland with some followers, landed on Iona and founded a monastery there. Before he died the whole of Scotland became Christian.

Julie Crocker is a rural Nebraska native. She likes the diversity of painting in different mediums including oil, acrylic, watercolor and gouache. She shares her talent with students and adults through her workshops. "Wildlife is one of my favorite subjects. I have spent many hours in the field observing, photographing and sketching. Painting in a realistic style, I try to create an interesting composition that is pleasing to the viewer and important to my work. It is the natural beauty of nature that inspires me to paint." Julie's work has been recognized nationwide and she has won many local and state awards. Some of her awards are: 1988–Nebraska "Artist of the Year" for Ducks Unlimited; 1993–"Award of Excellence," Fonner Grand Visions Art show; 1995–"Best of Show," Wings Over the Platte competition; Featured artist at the Imax Theatre during the opening of the Yellowstone Show (1995). She has taken top honors in the Nebraskaland Habitat Stamp Contest in 1993 and 1995. She also designed the Nebraska trout stamp for 1990, 1994 and 1996.

A vintage artist, **Mary Beth Dodson** is intrigued by an earlier era—its costumes, structures and antiques. She wrote the poem *Season of Cranes* immediately after her first experience of viewing the cranes from the privacy of a blind on the Platte River by Grand Island, Nebraska. "It was an experience I'll always remember." Mary Beth has a published book of poetry, *The Same Moon Rises*, and writes essays and fiction as well. Often she incorporates her prose or poetry into her paintings.

With the use of acrylic paints, **Cynthia Duff** enjoys weaving ribbons of colors to create a layered view of the plains and its inhabitants. Cynthia is a trained Commercial and Fine Artist who resides in Grand Island, Nebraska. She is very active in the Arts and is a member of Prairie Winds Art Center. Her works are in collections across the United States and have been featured in Nebraska Life Magazine, as well as having won numerous awards. "Art to me has been a journey of life and its spirit," says Cynthia.

Jessica Lyn Elkins, born in Oklahoma, raised as a preacher's kid in Texas, moved to New Mexico in 1968 with her husband and two preschoolers. Jessica earned a Bachelor of Arts in Geography and Biology in 1976 from the University of New Mexico and a Masters of Arts in Liberal Education from St. John's College in 1988. She has worked as a general contractor/builder and later as a human resources manager for multi-line auto dealers. Jessica grows herbs, watches birds, takes long walks, and writes from her North Valley home in Albuquerque.

Mirra Ginsburg is a well-known translator of many Russian and Slavic authors, including Mikhail Bulgakov and Yevgeny Zamyatin, as well as Isaac Bashevis Singer. Her translation of the *The Diary of Nina Kosterina* was widely acclaimed and selected as one of the best children's books of 1968 by the School Library Journal. She has also published *The Fox and the Hare*, a picture book retelling of a Russian folktale. Born in Russia, she has lived in Latvia and Canada and now, a citizen of the United States.

As a child growing up in the Platte River Valley around Columbus, Nebraska, **Loren Goedeken** gained a unique pleasure from outdoor activities. For whatever reason, he was fascinated with the beauty nature had to offer, whether it was a frosty sunrise or the remains of a tree stump fallen by beaver. To Loren, these scenes had a story to tell and a beauty worth remembering. It has been said that a picture is worth a thousand words. Words, even a thousand, could not describe the images set indelibly in his memory. Today the fascination, the inspiration, and the images still exist. And yet they are intensified by an eighteen-year absence from Nebraska. These years spent living in Montana, present among other natural beauties, inspired his brush strokes, but also increased his appreciation for the beauty of Nebraska landscape.

Han Shan, (date uncertain), means "Cold Mountain." It is not only the name of the place, but also the name of a person. Little is known for certain about the man who made that mountain his place of refuge, the symbol of his spiritual aspirations, and his own pseudonym. Possibly he lived in the early T'ang period. Probably he was a farmer who left his family from time to time to embark on obscure pilgrimages to Buddhist shrines or into the wilderness. In his poems he sometimes rants about the vanity of power, glory, wealth, and female beauty – all mere filth to him. But he could also write tenderly of misty peaks, bird songs, and the spiritual satisfactions of quiet and isolation. In these later times he was frequently represented in art as a freak in tattered garments, grinning imbecile, a happy social reject.

Han Yu, 768-824 AD, was born into a literary family of land gentry in Honan. His father died in 770 AD, and the young boy, age two, was raised in the family of Han Hui, a man of some reputation in literary circles. Han Yu was an instructor at the Imperial University, in 806 AD was promoted to a professorship at the university, and later made Rector of the University. After serving in several high posts in the government—Vice-president of the Ministry of War, Vice-president of the Ministry of Personnel, and Metropolitan Governor—he died in Ch'ang-an in 824 AD at age fifty-six. As a literary figure, Han Yu meets each of the requisites of a major poet: abundance, variety, and complete competence. His fame as a prose writer had unjustly overshadowed the high quality of his poetry. He was a daring innovator in both forms. His reform of Chinese prose style, the so-called *ku-wen* (ancient-style prose) movement, was totally accepted in the Sung, but debate continues to this day over the success of his innovations in poetry. The scope of Han Yu's poetry is vast; his major poems are long, making him a difficult poet to anthologize.

Humphrey Harman first went to Africa in World War II and spent most of his time with African soldiers in Africa, Madagascar, and the Far East. Africa seemed to him to be a good place to live and the people there good to live with. So, when the war ended, he became a schoolmaster, joined the Colonial Education Service, and went to Kenya, where he stayed for more than ten years. During that time, he served as a District Education Officer and trained African teachers in the area of Lake Nyanza. *Tales Told near a Crocodile* and *African Samson*, his first book to be published in the United States, are both based on stories told by the people of Nyanza.

Paula J. Harrington is a self-taught freelance photographer, specializing in nature and wildlife photography. She was born and raised on a farm in northeast Nebraska. It was there that she developed a love for wildlife and nature at an early age. She has expanded that interest through her photography. She hopes to capture on film the things that often go unnoticed by the average human eye. Nature is full of beauty and mystic and not everyone is able to visualize such magic. Her photography has become a means through which to share this beauty with others. Paula is currently a member of the Omaha Camera Club and the Fontenelle Forest Photographer's Club. She has won numerous awards in regional and national photo contests, has been published in several magazines and has prints displayed in collections throughout the United States and Europe. She can be reached at 2712 North 96th Drive; Omaha, Nebraska 68134.

About the year 110 BC a Chinese Princess named **Hsi-Chun** was sent, for political reasons, to be the wife of a century Asian nomad king, K'un Mo, king of the Wu-sun. When she got there, she found her husband old and decrepit. He only saw her once or twice a year, when they drank a cup of wine together. They could not converse, as they had no language in common.

Hsin Ch'I-Chi, 1140-1207 AD, was a hero in the last Sung wars against Chin aggression, possessed military knowledge and held both civil and army posts. He is considered the chief of the heroic school of *tz'u* writers.

Hsu Tsai-ssu, fl. 1300 AD, was a native of Chia-hsing, Chekiang. He wrote nothing but short lyrics. The two major categories of his lyrics are scenery and love. While his love poems are more or less conventional, he is sometimes capable of a realistic and colloquial style in presenting the lovers' psychology or in defining lovesickness. The immediacy of his lines adds much to Hsu Tsai-ssu's reputation as a love poet.

Huang Ching'jen, 1749 1783 AD, of Wu-chin (Ch'ang-chou), Kiangsu, was a fourteenth-generation decedent of the Sung poet Huang T'ing-chien. His family was poor, and he repeatedly failed the higher examinations after he won the *hsiu-ts'ai* degree in 1765. Though his poetic talents were recognized early by many leading scholars of his day, he remained depressed and impoverished all his life. At his death his friends raised money for his burial; the tragic circumstances of his life spread his poetic fame even further. Huang was also known for his painting and calligraphy.

Seeing is a question of perspective, **Sharon Jackson** brings a lifetime career of counseling, coupled with an extraordinary second sight to everything she sees. Dwelling deep in the woods, she lives in a turn of the century renovated log "speakeasy" that has a long history of dance bands and rolling dice. Her windows look out on families of deer, flocks of turkey, fox by moonlight, a glistening lake and a wide expanse of prairie from her home. Hidden in the camouflaged blind in her woods, she captures on film, each of the creatures she sees. Known in the Midwest area as an award winning photographer, her visions have graced walls from the cold of Alaska, the sun drenched homes of Laguna Beach, the forests of Maine and across the rolling ocean to Europe, the Mediterranean and the Middle East. Feature length presentations 30 feet tall of her nature photographs are seen daily in southern California by thousands of people a week at colleges and planetariums. All of Sharon's photographs are original, and not computer enhanced or digitally manipulated. Sharon states that "Reality is beautiful enough."

In a 1994 interview for Living Bird Magazine, **Paul Johnsgard** said that he had spent the first 30 years of his life learning how to become a scientist, and the next 30 trying to become a humanist and artist. Those efforts are reflected in his receipt of the Loren Eiseley Award from Omaha's Clarkson Hospital in 1988, given for writings that attempt to blend science with humanism, and the Mari Sandoz Award, given by the Nebraska Library Association in 1984 for contributions to the literature of Nebraska. Although Johnsgard has written for publication ever since he was an undergraduate at North Dakota State University in the early 1950s, it was not until twenty years later that he ventured into writing in a more literary style, and attempted to reach a much broader audience. This step has been accomplished in books such as *Song of the North Wind: A Story of the Snow Goose; Dragons and Unicorns, A Natural History; Those of the Gray Wind: The Sandhill Cranes; The Platte, Channels in Time; This Fragile Land: A Natural History of the Nebraska Sandhills; Earth, Water and Sky: A Naturalist's Stories and Sketches;* and *Prairie Children, Mountain Dreams.* In 1989 Nebraska Public Television produced a half-hour film on Johnsgard, titled *A Passion for Birds.* His books are distributed throughout the world and, through translations, are accessible to nearly half of the world's population.

Doug Johnson is an artist whose paintings have a similar visual effect as those of Monet and other impressionists. But rather than using the spontaneous brushwork of the impressionists, he uses numerous geometric shapes that fit together to form a intricate and detailed composition. Being a native Nebraskan, Doug concentrates his subject matter on the local landscape and native animals. His work is currently exhibited at the Warehouse Gallery in Grand Island, Nebraska, the University Place Art Center in Lincoln, Nebraska, and the Dakota Gallery in Rapid City, South Dakota.

Kasa Kanamura, Early Nara Period, was one of the members of the same family group to which the other notable Manyo poets such as Monk Manzei (or Kasamaro) belonged. The *Manyoshu* contains nearly fifty poems by him composed between 715 and 733 AD. He was a contemporary of Yamabe Akahito, and accompanied his Sovereign on various journeys. Many of his poems are panegyrics of the Imperial rule.

Anne Laurin learned the art of Japanese paper folding when she was thirteen from a Japanese student visiting her home in St. Louis, Missouri. Later, research in Japanese folklore introduced her to a Hokusai print, which combined with her knowledge of origami to inspire the *Perfect Crane*. A cultural anthropology major at UCLA, Ms. Laurin currently works in a Boston publishing house. Her first book, *Little Things,* published by Atheneum, was an ALA Notable Children's Book.

Aldo Leopold, 1886-1948 AD, American ecologist, born in Burlington, Iowa. He was an advocate for a "land ethic," in which humans see themselves as part of a natural community. After work in the U.S. Forest Service, he taught wildlife management at the University of Wisconsin and helped found the Wilderness Society. In 1924, he succeeded in having the Gila National Forest in New Mexico designated as the first extensive wilderness area in the United States. He wrote *A Sand County Almanac* in 1949, which helped provide the impetus to the environmental movement.

Pete Letheby is a native Nebraskan, born in Norfolk and now residing in Grand Island. He is married to Katrina and they have one son, one-year-old Alex. Pete is presently the associate editor of *The Grand Island Independent,* where his main duty is planning and designing special editions on a variety of topics. His primary interests / pursuits include writing, wildlife conservation and history, mainly Nebraska or regional history.

Jean Lewis has been photographing Nebraska for 20 years. She strikes out alone for a day or a week, her direction chosen by intuition. Sometimes she is compelled by the names of the places she has read about—Blue Hill, Weeping Water, Scalp Creek. Sometimes a story or a piece of folklore about a place intrigues Jean. Or maybe the ethnic connection is irresistible—the Bohemian Alps, the Russian Bottoms, or the Czech Capital of Nebraska. Jean has a briefcase crammed with topographical maps, state road maps, county road maps, maps drawn for her on matchbook covers, and maps she make s herself when she finds roads and landmarks unidentified elsewhere. Jean makes notes in the margins of the maps when she finds a place that she wants to see again – in another season, at another time of day – when the slant of light will be right. She reads all the local history books she can lay her hands on. Jean tries to find images that are distillations of the places and the people who have lived there. The sandhill cranes are a special love to her. She makes several daylong pilgrimages every year. Jean works with intensity since the cranes are in Nebraska for such a short time. Later, in the darkroom, she relives each wonderful, sacred experience.

Li Bai, 701-762 AD, was one of the greatest names in Chinese literature. It is believed he was born in central Asia and there is ample evidence to indicate that he moved with his family to Sichuan when he was five. At the age of 25 he began traveling in the hope of meeting people of influence who would help him to realize his political ambitions and ideals. In 742 he was summoned to the Tang capital. In 755, Li joined the loyalist forces led by Prince Yong in an attempt to resist the An Lushan rebels. When the Prince was defeated, he was banished to Guizhou. He regained his freedom when an amnesty was declared. He used the conventional verse forms of the day and his poetry, which frequently contains a strong element of fantasy and the supernatural, is known for its lyrical, innovative imagery and great beauty of language.

Poetess Li Ch'ing-chao, 1084?-c. 1151 AD, was a native of Li-ch'eng (modern Tsi-nan), Shantung, and lived in the intervening period between Northern Sung and Southern Sung. It may be said that she is one of the foremost lyric poets. Her happy marriage figures in most of her poems either actively celebrated or nostalgically recollected. The poetry of Li Ch'ing-chao reveals a mastery of language. Her attitudes are those of a woman, but her femininity is never servile or shrill. As a poet, she could be bold and delicate, languid and boisterous. Her attempt was to establish life in words: poetry was for her a stay against time, a surety to blot out oblivion. She tried to recapture the past, to preserve the present: in her own words, what she wanted to do was "still … hold onto a moment of time."

Li Ho, 791-817 AD, a native of Ch'eng'chi in Lung'hsi, Kansu. Born of hereditary privilege, he still managed to obtain a lowly position as Supervisor of Ritual at the Court of Imperial Sacrifices. He kept this position for three years, 811 to 814, and then, after a brief stay at his home, he joined the staff of one of the generals fighting a rebellious military governor. In 817 an illness caused him to return home, and he died shortly thereafter. Through his rich, allusion-laden poetry, Li Ho responded to his era. Because he was fond of using mythological themes and the shamanistic imagery of the *Ch'u Tz'u* in the same way that more traditional poets used nature and history as the source of their allusions, Li Ho has long been considered a mystic whose poems are obscure and even depressing. But this is not the case. Li Ho found in Taoist and shamanist sources congenial imagery, which allowed him to comment on the social and political evils of his day. His most mystical poems include the criticism of his own society, as do some of his less controversial poems.

Lu Kuei-meng, ?-c.881 AD, was born into a poor family in Ch'ang-chou (Wu-hsing) near Soochow, Kiangsu. Having failed many times in his attempts to pass the imperial examinations, Lu lived as a recluse in his native province. Lu seems to have found happiness only in boating through the beautiful Lake T'ai district, visiting temples and monasteries and practicing alchemy. An authority on tea, he was partially responsible for making that beverage an integral part of Chinese social life. His friends included P'i Jih-hsiu, to whom he dedicated most of his poems, Lo Yin, and other recluse poets. His nature poetry abounds in allusions to the texts of philosophical Taoism, and he is also known for his satirical prose in which he expresses his intense dislike of the vulgar people and harsh officials.

Mao Tse-Tung, 1893-1976 AD, was born into a well-to-do peasant family at Shao-shan in Hsiang-t'an, Hunan. Alternating between work at his father's farm and attending schools, he finally left home for Peking and Shanghai in his mid-twenties. In 1949, Mao became the chairman of the Central People's Government in the People's Republic. In addition to his political writings and polemics, he is also the author of some forty poems (most of the *tz'u* form). The poems have certain pronounced features. First, the poetry expresses a man's sentiments and beliefs—Mao's writings reflect the aspirations and ambitions of a political leader during the different periods of his career. Secondly, there is originality in his verses characterized by boldness in technical innovations or violations, as well as in his approach and outlook toward life. Lastly, his peculiar genius illuminates most of his best lines with imagination and sensitivity.

The poems in this book represent the first work **Anne McCollister** has written in 20 years. Cranes have enthralled her since she was a child. Her parents would release Anne from the car near Doc Peter's farm near Overton, Nebraska and they would race to find their traditional places on the banks of the Platte River before the sandhill cranes started flying in low just over the treetops to roost in the river. Each spring she still makes the pilgrimage to her favorite perch on the water and waits, takes notes, and listens to the chorus as it grows and grows when the cranes come in, all their number, to roost on the river's sandbars at dusk. "I am never ready to leave their (the crane's) lives and come back to my world. On those nights, I drive home slow."

Georgia McGuire has been a resident and a farmer's wife of the San Luis Valley, Colorado since 1933. She has numerous interests and hobbies including crochet, embroidery, quilt making, church and volunteer work, as well as gardening. Georgia wrote the poem "The Sandhill Cranes" when "I had been walking down a country road when a flock of cranes flew over head. [I] went home and wrote the poem that afternoon. My work is done strictly on inspiration of the moment."

Sergei Mikhalkov, one of Russia's best-loved writers of children's literature, was born in Moscow in 1913. He is the author of over six hundred books for children and adults, and his work has been translated into more than sixty languages. Several feature films have been based on his writings.

Doug Miller's initial start as a professional artist began in 1981 in Leavenworth, Washington, a beautiful Bavarian village on the east side of the Cascade Mountains. There, the rugged wilderness and the plentiful wildlife inspired many of his paintings. In 1994, he relocated in the desert expanses of central Washington; rock formation landmarks and the exotic, yet fleeting beauty of the desert flowers are reflected in Doug's most recent paintings. Born and reared on the plains of Kansas, Doug has a BA in art from Emporia State University. Doug believes his successful paintings are accomplished by spending hours observing nature. His love of the outdoors is reflected in his realistic attention to detail. Doug's work has been acknowledged for several awards and nominations. He was a top 100 finalist in the "Art for the Parks" competition for the years 1990 and 1995 in Jackson Hole, Wyoming, for two paintings include *The Olympic Rain Forest* and *Saguaro Scout*. He has been selected to create the thematic-design poster for the 1999 Wenatchee Apple Blossom Festival. The painting depicts a local landmark, Turtle Rock, located on the Wenatchee River, and features a family of Canada Geese in the shade of a blossoming apple tree.

Susan Milord is the author of *Tales Alive!*, *Tales of the Shimmering Sky*, *The Kids' Nature Book*, *Hands Around the World*, *Adventures in Art* and *Mexico!* She lives in Vermont.

Robert Morris began painting in January 1994. After receiving a set of professional watercolor paints from his children for Christmas, he felt compelled to try his hand at painting. It was at this point that a hidden talent was uncovered. Encouraged by family members and his wife Lynda, he continued to work at mastering a technique of applying his watercolor paints in a "tight, opaque manner." Unable to juggle a business career and give justice to his painting, he followed his heart, and became a full-time artist in June of 1995. As time progresses, so does the style that makes Robert Morris' paintings unique. Whether he is painting a serene garden setting or the portrait of some beautiful creature, his attention to depth and detail is amazing. This ability to stretch the watercolor medium is distinctly different from the techniques

243

taught in school and since he has had no formal training, each new painting is an adventure. Although Robert is just beginning to travel the art show circuit, his works of art are rapidly becoming popular. Art collectors from around the country have purchased originals, limited edition prints and commissioned pieces that are on display in their homes and offices.

Bob Moss is a devoted wildlife photographer. His goal is to "isolate and get as close to the subject as possible as well as safeguarding the subjects sanctuary and well being while capturing images that stir the imagination." Bob is a former aerial photographer and U.S. Air Force portrait photographer. He also was a TV news photographer for WOW-TV in Omaha, Nebraska. Bob began serious wildlife photography in the early 1990s and numerous newspapers and magazines alike have published his works. Bob Moss' work may be viewed on his web site, at the following address: www.members.xoom.com/bobmoss.

Osakabe Otomaro, the Fujiwara Period, no biographical data. Otomaro's *Manyoshu* contains only one poem by him, which was composed on the occasion of the journey of the Emperor Mommu to Naniwa.

Otomo Yakamochi, 718-785 AD, was the eldest son of Tabito. At the age of twenty-three he was appointed a court official in charge of palace-guards, and at twenty-nine Governor of Etchu Province, whence he returned to Nara in 751 as Junior Councillor of State. In 754 he entered the Department of War as an official of the 3rd rank. He was soon promoted to the post of Vice-Minister of War and then to Uchiben (bureau-chief in the Central Government); but relegated to Inaba Province as Governor in 758. Thenceforward he led a chequered career, marked, however, by frequent promotions and demotions. Finally he was appointed Senior Councillor of State and Steward to the Crown Prince, and was concurrently made Commander-in-chief of the Eastern Expeditionary Force. He died in 785. Shortly afterwards, because of a crime committed by a distant relative of his, not only was he posthumously deprived of his office and rank, but the great and ancient family of Otomo was broken up. Thus, the stormy vicissitudes of fortune that had attended his life followed him even beyond the grave. The large number of his poems in the *Manyoshu*, totaling about 500, were all composed before 759 when he was forty-two years old. It is supposed that his later works were all lost, though there might well have been many excellent verses emanating from a mind matured with age and experience. Nevertheless, Yakamochi who followed in the footsteps of Hitomaro, Akahito, and Okura, has left scores of good poems revealing his love of nature, tenderness, and loyalty, and profound insight into human affairs. His rare genius is manifested in the several tanka composed in 753 which represent the fine lyricism that characterized the poetry of the closing years of the Nara Period.

Charles A. Peek is a member of the faculty at the University of Nebraska at Kearney and an Episcopal priest. He and his wife Nancy live in Kearney, Nebraska, and are the parents of two grown children. Charles has won poetry awards for some of his poems, which have appeared in over twenty journals. Nebraska poets Don Welch and Charles Fort awakened his interest in writing about cranes. He can be reached at 2010 Fifth Avenue; Kearney, Nebraska 68847 or at capitan@nebi.com.

Carol Miles Petersen received her Ph.D. from the University of Nebraska. She taught English there as well as at the University of Nebraska – Omaha, and at Fremont Midland College. She is the author of the biography *Bess Streeter Aldrich, The Dreams Are All Real* and the editor of *The Collected Short Works, 1909 – 1919, The Collected Short Works, 1920-1954*, both by Bess Streeter Aldrich and both published by the University of Nebraska Press. Carol is also the editor of *Affectionately Yours* by Joyce Lierley, published by Making History Press.

P'i Jih-hsiu, c.833-883 AD, native of Hsiang-yang, Hupeh, was a recluse before he became an official in the chaotic years of the late Ninth Century. He earned his *chin-shih* degree in 867 and served on the staff of Ts'ui P'u, Censor of Soochow, when he became a friend of Lu Kuei-meng's. Ten years later, he was appointed Doctor of Letters in the Imperial University in Ch'ang-an. When the Huang Ch'ao rebellion broke out, he was captured, made to serve in the Hanlin Academy of the rebel government, and eventually killed. P'i Jih-hsiu's poetry, on the one hand, shows vast erudition (cf. *Thoughts in Early Autumn*) and on the other, incorporates realistic themes and everyday language (cf. *Orthodox Music Bureau Ballads*). In their simplicity, irony, and attention to detail, his verses foreshadow the development of Sung poetry.

Although **Sue Pickering** has always loved art, she recently began painting seriously, after her children were grown. What she hopes to show in her art is the beauty of simple things such as birds in flight, snow covered trees and light on water. Sue hopes people look at her painting and get lost in the serenity of nature. She celebrates the simple things in life.

Po Chu-I, 772-846 AD, was born at.T'ai-yuan in Shansi. Most of his childhood was spent at Jung-yang in Honan. His father was a second-class Assistant Department Magistrate. Chu-I stated that his family was poor and often in difficulties. Chu-I seemed to have settled permanently at Ch'ang-an in 801 AD. This town, lying near the northwest frontier, was the political capital of the Empire.

Marjorie Kinnan Rawlings, 1896-1953 AD, was an American author, born in Washington D.C., and a graduate of the University of Wisconsin in 1918. She was a journalist until 1928, when she moved to the Florida backwoods, where most of her novels are set. *Cross Creek* (1942) is a humorous autobiographical account of her life there. *The Yearling* (1938; Pulitzer Prize), is the story of a boy and his pet deer. Some of her other novels include *South Moon Under* (1933), *Golden Apples* (1935), and *The Sojourner* (1953).

Michael Rosen began writing for children in 1970, and since then his stories and poems have been published all over the world. Winner of the Smarties Prize in 1989 for *We're Going on a Bear Hunt*, he is a regular presenter of *Treasure Island*, a children's book program on BBC Radio. Mr. Rosen lives with his wife and five children in London, England.

Ralph T. Sanders is currently a full-time artist living in Santa Fe, New Mexico. He is a former professor of illustration and a public school graphic arts teacher. Sanders' artwork has been shown in numerous museums in the southeast United States. The images of herons and egrets are inspired from living in Tybee Island, Georgia, for a number of years. He has a Bachelor of Fine Arts and a Master of Fine Arts. Sanders can be reached at 2691 Via Caballero del Norte; Santa Fe, New Mexico 87505.

Donna Schimonitz-Leonard grew up on a dairy farm east of St. Paul, Nebraska. The farm provided Donna with ample livestock, horses, pets, and wildlife to observe, sketch, and respect. It was not unusual to be helping with farm chores and see a doe and her fawns grazing in the cornfield. A walk through the family woods had nature and wildlife foraging in every direction – from the tiny little nuthatch, to the soaring eagles above, the swimming turtles, to the gnawing beavers. Nature and its beauty drive her to capture these moments that Donna wants to enjoy longer than just one day. She wants to share these special opportunities, and their accompanying excitement—not store them away in just her heart and memories. Donna wants "to share their beauty and grace so others may also feel nature's importance as I do." *Ready to Roost* was created on a Macintosh computer using Macromedia Freehand software. Instead of using a pencil or brush, Donna drew the cranes with her "mouse."

The wonder of nature and the natural world has been a long-time interest for **Ward Schrack**. It probably started as he worked to become an Eagle Scout and as a counselor in summer camps then later a camp director. His specific interest in birds is traced to working on the Bird Study Merit Badge as a step in scouting. As a skilled photographer, Mr. Schrack has spent a lifetime photographing birds with particular emphasis on eagles and sandhill cranes. In more recent years he has been a very active environmentalist. He served two years as president of the Big Bend Audubon Society and later served professionally as a consultant to the National Audubon Society on issues of habitat preservation for crane migration. His home and workshop are located on what was at one time an island in the Platte River, near historic Ft. Kearney—right in the center of the sandhill crane migration route. Mr. Schrack has written *Shimingo: The Rites of Passage* and other books on birds for young people who are in the development stage. He is married, and he and his wife have four adult children.

Dorothea Hayward Scott, was a professional librarian, who spent many years in Mainland China, Hong Kong, New York and Wisconsin, USA. Her interest in cranes was inspired in the first place by the many beautiful examples of the crane in Chinese and Japanese art and literature and, later, in seeing for herself the dedicated work of the International Crane Foundation to save cranes everywhere. Mrs. Scott's books include *Chinese Popular Literature and the Child* and *A Fight of Cranes*.

Gerry Shepherd and her husband live in Kearney, Nebraska, and have three children and one grandchild. Born in Illinois, she has come to love the vastness of the Nebraska sky and beauty of the Platte River. Gerry works full time in real estate and is studying horticulture.

Su Shih, 1037-1101 AD, regarded by some as "the greatest of Sung poets," achieved pre-eminence in many fields which included *shis*, *tz'u*, belletristic prose, as well as calligraphy and painting. Born in Mei-shan, Szechwan, into a family of modest means did not win recognition as a scholar until the last decade of his life. Additionally his father, his brother, and Su Shih all became outstanding prose writers and poets of their age and were known as the Three Sus. Su Shih's checkered political career was marred by a series of defeats and banishment, primarily due to his opposition to Wang An-shih and also due to the acerbity of his writing, which at one time brought about his imprisonment. He was exiled to the provinces no fewer than twelve times. As a provincial administrator, he had the reputation of introducing benevolent policies and establishing a wonderful rapport with the people, especially in the area of public construction and relief work. From his experience in these various posts, he derived an immense knowledge of the lives of the common people, which was revealed in much of his poetry. Su Shih's works include over two thousand poems (*shih*) and over three hundred compositions in the lyric meter (*tz'u*). In either genre, he writes not only with great gusto but also with sufficient attention to the minutest details.

Ruth Tooze is widely known as a storyteller and author of many books. She developed the Children's Book Caravan as an adventure in showing children's books to teachers, parents, and children and talking about why we read and what we read. Mrs. Tooze remained with the Caravan for ten years and in 1958 made her first trip to Cambodia. Since that time she has traveled far and wide as both writer and lecturer, living in Ceylon and Cambodia with many trips to other Far Eastern lands, where she listened to and collected quantities of folk tales and folk lore.

Early in the Seventeenth Century **Edward Topsell** wrote a book, *The Fowls of Heaven* or *A History of Birdes* with a chapter on the *Crane*. Besides the most accurate description of cranes he could gather from information available at the time, he collected stories, poems and observations about cranes from ancient Greek and Roman writers as well as poems by Renaissance writers.

Tu Fu, 712-770 AD, has dominated Chinese literature for almost ten centuries as a master poet. He was the son of Tu Fan-yen, a high official in the T'ang Dynasty. Tu Fu came from a family of scholars, officials, and landowners, and rose early to a minor office in the court of Hsuan Tsung, called Ming Huang, the Bright Emperor. Although Tu Fu's young days were spent at Ming Huang's court, he became a Court Censor, a king of Tribune of the Patricians, under Su Tsung, Ming Huang's son. His last years were spent largely in a houseboat. All through his life Tu Fu wrote full dress poems of advise to the throne; full of wisdom. He was a member of the scholar gentry and suffered from their ethnocentrism and caste consciousness, however transfigured. Tu Fu was a valetudinarian. In the estimation of his countrymen he ranks next to Li Peh among the great poets of the T'ang Dynasty, and a few critics would give him a still higher place.

Tu Mu, 803-852 AD, poet and essayist, who was often referred to as "the Lesser Tu" as distinguished from Tu Fu, "the Greater Tu." He was born in Wan-nien in the Capital District *(Sian, Shensi)*, the scion of a distinguished family. When he was three years old, his grandfather Tu Yu (735-812) was ennobled as the Duke of Ch'i; a prominent statesman and scholar. Tu Yu was the compiler of the huge encyclopedia known as *T'ung-tien,* which contains the source material for the political and social history of China from the earliest time. A deep sense of the past pervades much of Tu Mu's own poetry. Tu Mu obtained his *chin-shih* degree in 828 and received appointments in the provinces. In the faction-ridden court of Emperor Wen-tsung, he served at one time as secretary to Niu Seng-ju (779-848), but he was never happy with either the Niu clique or that of Li Te-yu (787-850), Niu's chief rival. Thwarted in his political ambition to strengthen the royal house and restore it to the past glory, Tu Mu chose to pursue a life of pleasure in Lo-Yang , Yang-chou, and other metropolitan centers, and was known to be a connoisseur of beautiful women. In his poetry he prized himself for having shunned both the "ornate and the strange" on the one hand and "the commonplace and the vulgar" on the other. His own voice speaks most eloquently in his "regulated verse" poems and his quatrains; they are admired especially for their visual immediacy and delicacy of feeling.

Robert H. van Gulik entered the Netherlands Foreign Service in 1935. He had served in various posts in China, Japan, East Africa, Egypt, India, Lebanon and the United States. From 1965 until his death in 1967 he was the Netherlands Ambassador to Japan. A world-renowned orientalist, he has made a hobby of writing Chinese detective stories set in the time of the Tang Empire.

Valerie Vierk was born in Kearney, Nebraska, and has lived in south central Nebraska all her life. She has been writing since early childhood when she first put down her stories on yellow tablet paper. Valerie has been a member of the Nebraska Writer's Guild since 1988. She works as a secretary at the University of

Nebraska-Kearney and is a recent graduate with a BA in English. Valerie's short stories, poetry, and reminiscences have been published in *The Platte Valley Review, The Carillon, A Flowering a Festival, Nebraska Voice*, and several local and regional newspapers. She is presently working on two novellas that are set in Nebraska. Valerie loves nature, and this is often reflected in her writing as well as her daily life. She's in charge of a major project for the preservation of bluebirds in Ravanna, Nebraska, and a member of Bluebirds Across Nebraska (BAN). Photography is another of Valerie interests, and she has recently illustrated one of her works entitled *Three Christmas Stories from the Prairie* with pictures of her son, Edward.

Arthur Waley, 1889-1966 AD, was an English orientalist, born in London as Arthur David Schloss, and educated at Cambridge. He was and still is considered one of the world's greatest Asian scholars. Waley's most important works include his translations of Chinese poetry and of the Japanese novel, *The Tale of Genji* (1925-1933) by Murasaki Shikibu. Among his other works are *The No Plays of Japan* (1921), *The Poetry and Career of Li Po* (1959) and *The Secret History of the Mongols and Other Pieces* (1964). Waley never traveled to Asia.

Wang Shih-chen, 1634-1711 AD, was a native of Hsin-ch'ong, Shantung. He had a long and prominent career in the state bureaucracy, where he rose to the highest offices as President of the Censorate and President of the Board of Punishments. He is now remembered almost entirely as a literary figure - poet, essayist, critic, and anthologist. As a poet, Wang was especially attracted to the "serene and placid" landscape poetry of the Wang Wei tradition. But he also wrote in other styles as well; he was something of a "pluralist" who believed that there was a certain kind of poetry most appropriate for each human experience – serene contemplation, extreme emotion, homesickness, travel, narrative. Poetry for him was more an exercise in self-cultivation and an attempt to bring his own personal feelings into harmony with nature.

Wang Wei, 701-761 or 698-759 AD, was from Qixian County in Shanxi. He embarked upon an official career at an early age and in his later years retired to his country home in Lantian County, southeast of present-day Xi'an, China. A great painter and an accomplished musician, Wang for many represents the classical ideal of the cultured scholar-official. The majorities of his poems are about nature and are written in a restrained, exquisite and deeply symbolic style.

Art Washburn grew up in Denver, Colorado, graduated from Manual Training High School (as it was called then), received a BA from Reed College, Portland, Oregon, and a MS Ed. in the education of deaf children from Gallaudet University, Washington D.C. He went on to get his Ph.D. in education from Columbia. Art taught deaf children for 40 years. His poems have appeared in *Paper Gardens*, *Writers West*, and *Paws and Tales*.

Dr. Don Welch is a Reynolds Professor of Poetry, Emeritus at the University of Nebraska at Kearney, after a 38-year career in the University of Nebraska at Kearney's English Department. Dr. Welch is a life-long Nebraskan whose poetry reflects a deep sense of place in the landscape of the Great Plains. He has published books of poetry which included *Brief History of Fathers, Handwork, Fire's Tongue in the Candle's End, The Platte River, The Words Which Marry You to Me, Every Mouth of Autumn Says Goodbye*, and *The Plain Sense of Things*. He is a winner of the Pablo Neruda Prize for Poetry. As an educator, Dr. Welch received the Pratt-Heins and Nebraska State College Board of Trustees Awards for Teaching Excellence. He has been a Nebraska Arts Council poet-in-residence with Nebraska public schools and was a participant in and consultant to the Nebraska Public Television documentary *Last of the One-Room Schools*. His composition handbook, *A Shape a Writer Can Contain*, was published by the Nebraska Department of Education in 1979 and is still widely used in high school curricula throughout the state.

Wen T'ing-yun, 813?-870 AD, native of T'ai-yuan, Shansi, was well-known in his own times as an accomplished musician and man of letters. Caring little for Confucian standards of public morality and bureaucratic behavior, he performed badly in the civil service examinations, despite the name he enjoyed as an accomplished writer of the examination *fu* poetic style. A habitue of the cabarets and bordellos, which flourished in the large metropolitan centers, he developed a reputation for irresponsible and unmannered behavior. That environment, with its popular music and song, contributed to his development as a poet. Wen T'ing-yun is most often thought of as a *tz'u* poet because of his important contributions to the early development of that form. His *shih* poetry, which is also richly varied in theme, manner, and diction, is however no less interesting.

Cheryl J. Wilkinson of Oshkosh, Nebraska, is a representational acrylic and watercolor artist. Her paintings are honest and sincere stemming from her love of nature and home. Her family heirlooms are used in her still life. The thousands of wild geese that roost near her barn in winter, deer, coyotes and other wildlife on her river ranch give her the incentive to paint wildlife. Cheryl says, "I believe God gave me the talent to paint and to write and I must keep striving to do better whether I'm wielding the brush or the pen." She attended Chadron State College and retired after twenty-five years of teaching school. Cheryl has exhibited locally, regionally, and nationally, winning many awards.

Yamabe Akahito, 710-784 AD, Early–Middle Nara Period. Little is known of the poet save that, accompanying the Emperor Shomu, he traveled over various provinces. He is unsurpassed in tanka, his long poems being comparatively brief. In contrast to Hitomaro, the poet of passion, Akahito wrote nature poems marked with limpidity and grace of style. His poem on Mount Fuji is one of the best known of his works. With Hitomaro, he has been known as a "Saint of Poetry."

Yun-k'an Tzu, date unknown, is the religious pseudonym of an otherwise anonymous Taoist recluse who lived in the first half of the Fourteenth Century. His work of twenty-seven short poems, written in the *ch'u* form, is in many ways similar in content to the *shih* poetry of the famous T'ang Buddhist poet Han Shan.

Additional Reading

The Crane by Gabriel Horn

Cranes of the World by Paul A. Johnsgard

Cranes of the World by Lawrence Walkinshaw

The House of Wings by Betsy Byars

In Search of a Sandhill Crane by Keith Robertson

The Japanese Crane: Bird of Happiness by Dorothy Britton and Tsuneo Hayashida

The Sandhill Cranes by Lawrence H. Walkinshaw

Sandy: The True Story of a Rare Sandhill Crane Who Joined Our Family by Dayton O. Hyde

Snow Country and Thousand Cranes by Yasunari Kawabata

So Cranes May Dance by Barbara Katz

Sunflower Splendor, Three Thousand Years of Chinese Poetry by Wu-chi Liu and Irving Yucheng Lo

To Africa with the Migratory Bird by Bengt Berg

Those of the Gray Wind: The Sandhill Cranes by Paul A. Johnsgard

Valley of the Cranes by Rozinski, Shattil, and Simmons

The Whooping Crane: The Bird that defies Extinction by F. McNulty

Index by Artist

Index by Author

Index by Title

To purchase *Legends of the Crane* contact:

Sandstones
4996 Eugene Court
Denver, Colorado 80239
303-574-9070

Pjjensen3@juno.com